The life of Berlioz

Musical lives

The books in this series will each provide
an account of the life of a major composer,
considering both the private and the public
figure. The main thread will be biographical,
and discussion of the music will be integral
to the narrative. Each book thus presents an
organic view of the composer, the music,
and the circumstances in which it was written.

Published titles

The life of Berlioz

PETER BLOOM

CAMBRIDGE
UNIVERSITY PRESS

PUBLISHED BY THE PRESS SYNDICATE OF THE UNIVERSITY OF CAMBRIDGE
The Pitt Building, Trumpington Street, Cambridge CB2 1RP, United Kingdom

CAMBRIDGE UNIVERSITY PRESS
The Edinburgh Building, Cambridge, CB2 2RU, United Kingdom
40 West 20th Street, New York, NY 10011-4211, USA
10 Stamford Road, Oakleigh, Melbourne 3166, Australia

© Cambridge University Press 1998

First published 1998

Printed in the United Kingdom at the University Press, Cambridge

Typeset in FF Quadraat 9.75/14 pt, in QuarkXPress™   [SE]

A catalogue record for this book is available from the British Library

Library of Congress cataloguing in publication data

Bloom, Peter.
The life of Berlioz / Peter Bloom.
  p.   cm. – (Musical lives)
ISBN 0 521 48091 4 (hardback) – ISBN 0 521 48548 7 (paperback)
1. Berlioz, Hector, 1803–1869.   2. Composers – France – Bibliography.
1. Title.   II. Series.
ML410.B5B58   1998
780′.92–dc21   98–3050 CIP

ISBN 0 521 48091 4 hardback
ISBN 0 521 48548 7 paperback

for Catherine, Alexandra, and Caroline

CONTENTS

ILLUSTRATIONS

Grateful acknowledgment is made for the use of illustrations from the following sources: Musée du Louvre (front cover, 3); Photothèque des Musées de la Ville de Paris (2, 6, 7, 11, 12): Bibliothèque Nationale de France (5, 8, 9, 10, 15); Archives Nationales de France (14); Smith College (4, 13, 16).

ACKNOWLEDGMENTS

My understanding of French culture has long been deepened by conversation at table with my in-laws, M. et Mme André Marchiset, to whom I should like to express my most affectionate gratitude for many kindnesses over many years.

My interest in Berlioz was sparked in the nineteen-sixties by reading *Berlioz and the Romantic Century* and it has been fueled for some thirty years by correspondence with that monumental book's author, Jacques Barzun, whose graceful and erudite replies to my queries have provided me with a rare, private education. For almost as long I have shared enthusiasms with Hugh Macdonald, the editor of Berlioz's complete musical works, David Cairns, Berlioz's modern biographer, and D. Kern Holoman, Berlioz's "Köchel." The friendliest possible exchanges with my colleague in France, Joël-Marie Fauquet, have helped me to focus the lens through which I view Berlioz in this book. And discussion at home and abroad with my dear friend and distinguished colleague on the faculty at Smith College, Hans Rudolf Vaget, has been a source of tremendous pleasure and enlightenment. Because the series in which this book appears eschews the sort of finicking footnotes I have always been predisposed to furnish, I should like here globally to acknowledge my profound debt to these scholars' editions, books, articles, reveries, and reviews.

I owe a very special debt of gratitude to my eminent teacher of long ago, John de Lancie, whose artistry has been one of the great musical inspirations of my life. For support of a more practical sort, I am grateful to my old friend Dennis Alter, whose *largesse* has lately helped me to spend time in Berlioz's homeland without fear (often experienced by Berlioz and his contemporaries) of being incarcerated for debt.

It is a pleasure to mention other friends and colleagues who have offered advice and assistance of various sorts, among them Katherine Kolb, H. Robert Cohen, Ralph Locke, Denis Herlin, Miriam Rosen, Brian Burrell, Élisabeth Valsamis, Dorothy Eckel, Javier Roca, and Franklin Lloyd Kochman.

For sharing with me her knowledge of her country's language and culture, I am especially happy to acknowledge my long-suffering wife, Catherine Marchiset Bloom: Berlioz would be proud of her for quipping, in response to my acquisition of French citizenship during the writing of this book, that I *did not deserve it*. It is true that I, like my Anglo-Saxon *confrères* who have written on Berlioz, will always remain the *naïf voyageur* in France. In my defense, and in theirs, I can only cite the simple words of the Russian poet Joseph Brodsky, exiled in America: "It takes a stranger to see some things clearly."

"Beethoven!" most people will exclaim when asked, impromptu, to name a composer. "Berlioz, *hélas*," is what my wife and children would say. This book is lovingly dedicated to them.

Introduction

Fantastique – the expressive and euphonious title of his astonishing first symphony – has for too long stood in the popular imagination as emblematic of Berlioz's life: a fantastical love story, passionate, even ecstatic, yet at the same time tormented, and inescapably doomed. Berlioz may have wanted it this way, for the susurrations of everyday life do not give birth to music of high drama, and the author of memoirs more spirited than those of any other musician was nothing if not a purveyor of dramatic action and emotion. Further, people become what others remember of them, and many remembered Berlioz as discouraged – as he often was, of course, but as he more often painted himself in letters and autobiographical writings of great poignancy and range. We have to attempt to distinguish the sometimes melancholic "orchestration" of his self-portraits from the essence, no small task when orchestration, as it always seems to be in Berlioz, is *of* the essence.

Still, if his work, his modes of behavior, and his categories of judgment were conditioned by his artistic endeavors, they were also conditioned by well developed social forces and institutions – the family, the church, and especially the state – which provided his education and shaped his experience. Knowledge of his culture, then, even if we can never know the real Berlioz, will bring us closer to the creator of the *Symphonie fantastique*, of *La Damnation de Faust*, and of the other intimate and monumental works of dramatic expression and unconventional structure that cause us, now, to view him as the finest composer of the French nineteenth century; it will bring us closer to the director of scores of orchestras across the European continent who eventually dominated the still youthful profession of orchestral conducting, and to the author of a brilliant autobiography and of many hundreds of newspaper and magazine reviews that clearly established him as the leading music critic of his generation.

Looking from the outside in, I have come to think that the reality of his life was often brighter than the dark colors of so many reminiscences, including his own. I touch upon this matter here, among others, in three chapters that treat, in loosely chronological order, Berlioz's reactions to the political goings-on of his time, his professional activities, his financial affairs and affairs of the heart, and his letters, books, and articles. Each chapter includes brief mention of some of the music composed in the period under consideration and some of the issues that that music urges us to weigh. In an Afterword I draw some comparisons with the imposing figure of Richard Wagner, who dominated the second part of the century, and who refracts – as Beethoven does the first – our image of the period as a whole.

Three-ness persists in the musical arena as a notion well suited to the organization of the creative life of the artist. In this book, I have adapted to Berlioz the three-fold division widely employed (and debated) in writings about Beethoven's life and work, using as partitions the two revolutionary upheavals of 1830 and 1848, which left clear lines in the historical record. The words I assign to the trinity of Berlioz's youth, maturity, and seniority, it should be understood, are intended playfully to suggest, and not eternally to define, salient aspects of our composer and his craft.

"Initiation" replaces the word "imitation," which was originally applied to the first of Beethoven's three periods by the French composer Vincent d'Indy, who then went on to speak of Beethoven's periods of "externalization" and "reflection." Berlioz did see himself as a disciple of Gluck and Spontini, and he did call his first Mass a "clumsy imitation" of his teacher, but no work of his ever followed a model the way some of Beethoven's deliberately followed Mozart's. Like Wagner, Berlioz was poetically inspired by Beethoven, and took over something of the great German composer's bearing as a temperamental genius, but he had a thirst for novelty that never permitted him to be an imitator. "Initiation" seems a better word to suggest what the young man underwent when he arrived in Paris as a well-educated lad from the provinces, with limited musical training and no big-city experience, prepared to follow the footsteps of his father and become a country doctor, but smitten by the excitement of the opera during what must have been a period of intense emotional conflict, and ultimately seduced by the promise of a life in the arts.

Berlioz was awarded the Prix de Rome in the immediate aftermath of the three-day revolution of July 1830, and the première of his still most widely celebrated work, the *Symphonie fantastique*, was given as the ministers of the deposed Bourbon monarch went on trial for their lives. These things represent a felicitous confluence of art and politics rarely found by the historian looking for a not-too-artificial divide. The prize and the symphony symbolize the completion of the apprenticeship and the coming-out of a composer who had already produced works of substance, but who would create, in the following decade, a series of works of unparalleled imagination and ambitious design. For this, the Beethovenian term "externalization" would have served perfectly well. But I apply "innovation" as a way of underlining the manifest self-consciousness of Berlioz's choices, in the face of inherited traditions, in the first years of his full maturity as a composer.

"Introspection," too, can apply to all manner of Berlioz's work, for he was a conspicuously premeditative craftsman. I use the word to accentuate the fact that it was in the midst of the revolutions of 1848 that he, like Chateaubriand after 1830, undertook the quintessentially introspective task of writing a volume of *Mémoires* – whose Preface, dated 21 March 1848, suggests, with more than a touch of melancholy, that "the art of music, for so long everywhere hanging on for dear life, is at this hour no more." Jules Massenet opened his own autobiography with a similar dramatic gambit, affixing to its first page the date of the abdication of Louis-Philippe, 28 February 1848. (The further revolutions of that year moved Richard Wagner to introspection, too, and soon thereafter to start to forge *The Ring*.)

We can detect in and around 1848 something of a caesura in Berlioz's musical style as well, for the energies necessitated by the extroverted conclusion of the *Te Deum* (completed in 1849, although conceived well before the outbreak of hostilities) were for Berlioz like those of completing a final novel. As he told his sister on 1 September 1849, you are all the happier writing the last chapter of such a book because you swear to yourself that you will never again write another. The work that did eventually follow, after a creative hiatus of some three years, was the decidedly more intimate *L'Enfance du Christ*. Unlike Beethoven, however, whose distinctive late style has at times been seen as a "critique" of his earlier manner, Berlioz underwent no such clear shift of perspective. His final works – like Mozart's, really – derive from what seems to be an urge at once to deepen and to simplify, to classicize and to refine.

Berlioz's death, too, came at what might be described as the end of an era, as it occurred within a year of the deaths of Rossini, Lamartine, Sainte-Beuve, Mérimée, and others of the French romantic generation to whom Gustave Flaubert referred when he wrote to George Sand, on 13 March 1869 (five days after Berlioz's death), that there had been "a frightful lot of dying this winter!" Berlioz would surely have had mixed feelings about the Franco-Prussian War, which broke out sixteen months later, for, *Bonapartiste* though he may have been, many of his triumphs had occurred on the far side of the Rhine, and among others, the former King of Prussia, Frederick William IV, had been personally generous to him.[1] Still, if illness and old age had not already taken their toll in 1869, the collapse of 1870 and the Commune of 1871 might have done it – or so the zealous periodizer might be led to suggest.

My use of a three-fold division was encouraged by Berlioz's own acceptance of this sort of useful fiction. In a biographical sketch of

Beethoven that appeared in the short-lived Parisian magazine *Le Correspondant*, on 11 August 1829, Berlioz wrote that Beethoven's works "should be divided into three distinct classes related to the three principal epochs of his life." This is one of the earliest appearances in print of such a notion, which is usually attributed to the Russian writer Wilhelm von Lenz, who had the excellent idea, at a time when books were judged by their covers, to publish one in 1852 entitled *Beethoven et ses trois styles* (*Beethoven and his Three Styles*).[2] Still, as we know from later writings, Berlioz was well aware of the fallible if seductive nature of such a well-ordered framework for the observation of what is in actuality through-composed data.

Most of those who have admired Berlioz have seen him primarily as the composer of his music and as the author of his prose – the identity he would naturally privilege himself. But it is equally important to understand Berlioz in his identity as a French subject, in monarchy and empire, and as a French citizen, in revolution and republic. Berlioz lived as an artist in a country where it was and is still commonly said that it is the state that makes the man, and not the man who makes the state. Such a person, a member of a cultural class ambiguously intermingled with the class in power, would of necessity have to deal often not only with princes and kings, but with ministers and clerks, and with civil servants and lesser mandarins who were themselves individuals of human sensibilities and not simply anonymous pawns on the chessboard of the establishment. We tend to see the directors of the government-supported Opéra in Paris, for example, and of the government's bureau of fine arts, as so many inanimate deterrents to the flowering of Berlioz's genius. But to try to know him, we must try to know them, too.

Indeed, Berlioz dedicated his Opus 1 to the government's Directeur des Beaux-Arts, and he dedicated a host of further works to princes and potentates at home and abroad. Such dedications show a respect for authority that extends beyond political expedience, for Berlioz surely hoped that these nobles and Royals would approach his works on the basis of the artistic training they would have had, as individuals of aristocratic standing, to appreciate the finer things in life. It is not that elite station guaranteed a refined taste for elite music, of course, for those best qualified to follow the intricacies of Berlioz's music were his fellow musicians – the composers, players, and singers whom he knew, coached, and admired. It is rather that such station afforded the possibility of leisurely contemplation and attentive audition – precisely what Berlioz always believed that good music required. (Wagner, too, that erstwhile revolutionary, came to decry the philistine values of the bourgeois public and the "caprices" of "Parisian" taste.)

In Wagner scholarship, it is common for the author of each new study to offer a witty apologia for his work in the form of a reference to the enormous quantity of books and articles already devoted to the subject, a quantity rivaled only by publications associated with Napoleon Bonaparte and Jesus Christ. In modern Berlioz scholarship we have no such problem – although the appearance in 1982 and 1989 of biographies by three major Berlioz scholars (Hugh Macdonald, David Cairns, and D. Kern Holoman) does suggest that some justification for this one is needed. Suffice it to say that the present book is decidedly more limited in scope and intent than those of my colleagues, and aspires only to project for the general reader some of the principal issues and episodes in the life of the artist.

Berlioz scholars are fortunate that one of the composer's great mid-century advocates has lived into the late nineteen-nineties, helping many of us who have come along in his footsteps to keep on the right track. Jacques Barzun's grand cultural history of 1950, *Berlioz and the Romantic Century*, continues to be a model of scholarly excellence. That this French-born author's work never appeared in French is the reason that the impressive but strangely wavering biography by Adolphe Boschot, which began to appear in 1906, was so long considered definitive in the composer's native land.[3] French readers may now turn to Henry Barraud's useful and non-technical volume of 1955. They may also turn to recent translations of the books by

Holoman and Cairns, for French Berliozians are still rare, and non-French scholars remain in the forefront of Berlioz research.

Inspired by his work, musical *and* literary, and in particular by the new critical editions of his scores and letters, we write of Berlioz because to do so, hopeful of casting light along the way, is ultimately to relive pleasures past and present. Ought we to apologize for a particular interest in the biography, as though interest in the music were of some sort of *moral* superiority? Here the *Catalogue of the Works of Hector Berlioz*, Holoman's splendid achievement, suggests an answer: unique among such volumes, it urges Berlioz's correspondence and other writings upon us with nearly the same force as it does the music. Those writings demonstrate a central tenet of the romantic era – the conscious interweaving of artistic invention and personal history – and a central fact of Berlioz's artistic existence – the heavy burdens placed upon the creator by the demands of real life. These differ from, but impinge upon, the demands of art.

A closing word about sound and image. We have ample evidence, pictorial and descriptive, of Berlioz's appearance; we know that his conversation was now shy and restrained, now impassioned and eloquent; but we know little of the sound of his voice, and cannot be certain of how he pronounced his name. In M.-A. Lesaint's *Traité complet de la prononciation française* (1850), it is specifically said that the z in the name *Berlioz* is articulated, though rather less forcefully than the z at the beginning of a word (such as z*è*bre). This surely accounts for those instances in nineteenth-century writings where we find the final z replaced by an *s*. There is some indication, however, that in his own day, Berlioz did hear his name without the terminal consonant. On occasion he was confused in the press with a friend, the violinist Charles de Bériot, whose t was silent. More pertinently, the rebus that Jean-Pierre Dantan affixed to his caricature-statuette of the composer in 1836 – the letters BER followed by a bed (lit) raised above the ground (*haut*) (see illustration 7) – demonstrates that the z was sometimes not pronounced. Still, it seems best to do as most of the natives do now, and thus to sound the z.[4]

As for pictures: both Cairns and Holoman use on the dust jackets of their biographies the brilliant portrait of Berlioz by his fellow Roman traveler Émile Signol, the French Academy's prize-winning painter in 1830 (see illustration 5). The portrait was completed in the spring of 1831, but it is marked 1830 to suggest the Berlioz of the incipient legend, the Berlioz of the Prix de Rome and of the *Fantastique*, the Berlioz of the year of the *bataille d'Hernani* provoked by Victor Hugo's iconoclastic play, the Berlioz of the year of Delacroix's now celebrated *La Liberté guidant le peuple*. This painting, titled *le 28 juillet* in honor of that tumultuous day of the July Revolution, has been reproduced in the history manuals of generations of French children and has become in some ways a visual symbol of France itself. It is because of my wish to underscore Berlioz's inevitable engagement with the social and political upheavals of his time, and because of my belief that Berlioz's art is equally symbolic of the artistic capabilities of the nation, that I give pride of place, on the cover of this book, to Delacroix's *Liberté*.

In the little-known photograph taken in the mid-eighteen-fifties by Gaspard-Félix Tournachon, known to all as Nadar (see illustration 12), we see the firm gaze so characteristic of the composer, the gentle hand, the ever-present ribbon of the Légion d'honneur, and the silken cravat tied with an air of *insouciance* that renders our man both dapper and worldly-wise. Here, too, is an image that I should like to stress: a non-caricatural Berlioz, a cosmopolitan Berlioz whose international travel and acclaim never weakened his deep-seated love of country, a Berlioz who would occupy an ordinary place in the pantheon of those extraordinary few who endowed western music with monuments that continue to give sound meaning to those who would listen.

1   Initiation (1803–1830)

A childhood of learning and love

Berlioz once ridiculed Wagner and the Germans for taking birthdays so seriously, and always minimized the importance of his own. As a toddler he would have learned the official place and date of his birth not as La Côte-Saint-André, 11 December 1803, but as La Côte-Bonne-Eau, 19 Frimaire An XII. A decade earlier, during the great Revolution, the authorities had abolished royalty and instituted a calendar intended to celebrate the advent of a newly dechristianized age of reason. It was in accord with the then prevailing ideology, which preferred the names of classical heroes to those of the saints, that Berlioz was always called Hector, despite the *Louis-*Hector of his baptismal certificate. The ideology may have been little accepted at La Côte, but Berlioz's father adopted its trappings, and presumably tried to impress their significance upon his son. The rites of religion returned to La Côte in the early days of the new century, and the Republican calendar was officially annulled at the end of 1806. But stories of the Revolution and its aftermath, centering upon the titanic figure of Napoleon Bonaparte, must have been the stuff of Berlioz's childhood, despite his mother's efforts to steer him towards religious faith. "Needless to say," he would write on the opening page of his *Mémoires,*

> I was brought up in the Catholic and Apostolic Church of Rome. This charming religion (so attractive since it gave up burning people) was

for seven whole years the joy of my life, and although we have long
since fallen out, I have always kept most tender memories of it.[1]

More crucial to his mature compositions, however, was the notion of
bold and tragic majesty that would naturally have been associated
with the man who rose and who fell as Emperor of France during the
first ten years of the boy's life.

Berlioz was a newborn infant when the French flag was lowered
over New Orleans, after Thomas Jefferson's Louisiana Purchase initiated a giant step westward for the new American Republic; and he was
only eleven at the time of the catastrophe at Waterloo, in 1815. But he
was eighteen when the news of Napoleon's death reached France in
1821, and one may fairly wonder – since he later wrote a "grand and
sad" cantata to commemorate the event – whether this impressed him
even more than those intense moments of the subsequent Restoration
that were the death of Louis XVIII, in 1824, and the coronation of his
successor, Charles X, in 1825. Still, it is clear that the first political
event which he believed would have a direct effect on his career was the
revolution that ended the reign of Charles X in the waning days of July
1830 – the revolution commemorated in the famous poster painting
by Eugène Delacroix that became the image of the democratic impulse
in France.

The playwright Ernest Legouvé, who knew Berlioz for over three
decades, said that love was the alpha and omega of his existence. The
assessment, if exaggerated, is not unfair. When Berlioz was a preco-
cious twelve-year-old, he became hopelessly infatuated with a girl
from a nearby village who was four years older than he. For the rest of
his life, he continued to think of her as a kind of ideal – as the *Stella del
monte* or star of the mountain "whose radiant beauty," he wrote in
1848, "illuminated the morning of my life." Estelle Dubœuf became
the untouched target of his amorous yearning, a true distant beloved,
and the object of his fantasy – even though the life she later led as wife
to a judge in Grenoble, Casimir Fornier, and as mother to four chil-

dren, was ordinary in the extreme. Berlioz always saw her through rose-colored lenses, whose tint was deepened by a name that echoed Florian's *Estelle et Némorin*, the pastoral novel (with its own tales of the despondency of young love) that Berlioz read and reread as a teenager. The real Estelle,

> the Estelle I am speaking of, was a girl of eighteen with a tall, elegant figure, large eyes ready for the attack (though they were always smiling), a head of hair that would have graced Achilles' helmet, and the feet, I will not say of an Andalusian, but of a pure-bred Parisian, clad in little pink boots!

He came to know the real Estelle again in old age, and he let her know that she had long been the inspiration for the amorous scenes of his music, whose pleasures, at twelve, he was just beginning to experience. Thus the extreme feelings and sensitive admixtures of art and life that characterize Berlioz's entire existence took shape here, in the hills outside Grenoble, where the pre-adolescent boy adored the smile and budding femininity of his glowing summer companion.

It was at home that Berlioz received his basic education, largely from his intelligent and methodical father, Louis-Joseph, who had completed his own training as a medical doctor only months before his marriage to Antoinette-Joséphine Marmion, in February 1803, and only a year before the birth of his first son, Hector, in December of that year. Taking advantage of the law of 1811 that permitted candidates for the *baccalauréat ès lettres* to be educated outside official institutions, and initiating what was more commonly done for female children, Louis Berlioz instructed his son in his own large house on the main road of La Côte (now home to a Berlioz museum) – in Latin, French, geography, and anatomy. He employed tutors for the teaching of mathematics and dance, but he put forth the rudiments of music to the boy himself, with the assistance of Berlioz's uncle, Félix Marmion, who was a great music lover, and who supervised the child as he learned the names of the notes. There was no opera or serious instrumental music in his sleepy hillside town, so whatever musical appetite Berlioz had in

1 A view from the courtyard of Berlioz's paternal home, now the Musée Hector
Berlioz, at 69, rue de la République, La Côte-Saint-André.

those early years had to be satisfied by the celebratory fanfares of the
band of the region's National Guard, and by the liturgical chant that
was sung in the local church.

To describe Berlioz's situation at this time one could use the language of the most celebrated composer at the dawn of the new century, Joseph Haydn, who said of his experience at the country
residence of his patron-prince that, because it was set apart from the
"world," it had forced him "to become original." Berlioz's situation
was nothing like that of the older master, of course, but the words
seem apt. Far from the big city, he learned to coordinate breath and
fingers on the flageolet (a first cousin to the recorder) and, with lessons from a teacher from Lyon, to sight-read, to sing, and to play the
flute well enough eventually to manage a demanding concerto. He
began to practice the guitar when he was fifteen or sixteen years old
and soon became quite adept on the instrument, of which the six-
stringed variety was then coming into general use in Europe.

Around the same time Berlioz made his first experiments in
composition, inspired by reading the biographies of Gluck and
Grétry, aided by hearing some quartets by Ignaz Pleyel, and groping
on his own with the help of theoretical treatises by Rameau and Catel.

Our knowledge of this part of Berlioz's life is scanty, however (David Cairns's narrative of the period is as thorough as is ever likely to be produced), and the musical remains – some *romances* and music for guitar – are too few to impress. Still, there is sufficient evidence to suggest, in hindsight, that the boy might have been seen as a prodigy had his talent been encouraged by a father such as Leopold Mozart. It was medicine, however, not music, that mattered most to his father, and that consequently had to matter to him.

The medical student

Though Louis Berlioz must have found Hector a hungry pupil, and must have been gratified by the appetite for science and literature that he had instilled in his son (who throughout his life read the classics and the moderns with equal enthusiasm), he never warmed to Berlioz's chosen career. The composer may well have owed his inquisitive mind to the instruction he had received at home from his father, but he was clearly saddened by the painful reality that the old man never rid himself of his provincial prejudice against the arts – a prejudice which presumably saw the practice of music as appropriate primarily to women.

Berlioz persevered in his academic studies and, on 22 March 1821, in Grenoble (fifty kilometers southeast of La Côte), at age seventeen (one year above the minimum), he was awarded the *baccalauréat ès lettres* – a social passport and a key to the doors of a number of professional careers – by passing an oral examination that consisted essentially of an *explication de texte* in Latin. At the end of October he began the four- or five-day coach ride to Paris with his cousin, Alphonse Robert, there to enroll in the Faculty of Medicine and to pursue – willingly, we must presume, at least at first – the career chosen for him by his father.

The Paris that Berlioz encountered was a rapidly growing nineteenth-century city still set in an essentially medieval framework. Most accounts give us a crowded, noisy, muddy, and unappetizing place where relief could be had only from the clear air and clean water, the moderate climate, and the general excitement of the environment. The hubbub was heated by the newspapers, one more partisan than the next, and by the journalists – some professionals who said what they meant and meant what they said, others (as we know from Balzac's *Les Illusions perdues*) hacks whose critical favors were easily bought and sold. (If another of Balzac's tales, *Gobseck*, is to be believed, women were actually shielded from the inanities reported in the newspapers.) Still, the periodical press was the principal means of public communication at the time, and when Berlioz later became a journalist, he would acquire a voice and a visibility that were elsewhere unmatched.

On 16 November 1821, equipped with his *baccalauréat*, Berlioz registered as a student at the Faculté de Médecine of the Académie de Paris of the Université Royale de France – that is, at the medical school of the Paris campus of the nation-wide university system. In chapter 5 of his *Mémoires* – a book that shows a decided preference for eye-witness accounts and skilled exercises in ventriloquism – Berlioz gives us the flavor of his experiences as a young medical student, including his first visit to the dissection room of the Hospice de La Pitié:

> At the sight of that terrible human ossuary – the limbs scattered
> about, the heads smirking, the skulls gaping, the bloody cesspool
> underfoot, the repulsive stench of the place, the swarms of sparrows
> fighting over scraps of lung, the rats in the corner gnawing on
> bleeding vertebrae – such a feeling of revulsion possessed me that I
> took off at top speed, jumped through the window of the arena, and
> ran home gasping as though Death himself and all his grisly band
> were hot on my heels.

The next day, Berlioz tells us, he was somehow cured, and able to face the place with nothing but a cold disgust. Was it as horrible as he describes? Did he really jump through the window? For American doctors of that day, Paris was a center of medical science, a medical "Mecca," with its several hospitals providing clinical material for students that was rarely available in the United States. One American visitor noted the relative neatness of the dissection rooms that so revolted Berlioz; another mentioned the maternity wards that were closed to students because of the attractions of the midwives: the young doctors there, it appears, had a tendency to "make more babies than they delivered."[2]

After two years of sometimes troubled study, during which he seems at least momentarily to have considered studying the law, Berlioz passed the examination that led to his being awarded, on 13 January 1824, the diploma of *bachelier-ès-sciences physiques* – the degree that medical students, following the directives of 1823, were required to have.[3] Given his increasingly time-consuming musical enthusiasms, it is remarkable that he was able to prepare the oral examinations required for this degree – in mathematics, physics, chemistry, zoology, botany, and mineralogy. His life gives plenty of evidence of his intelligence, but he must have been a quick student, capable of working efficiently on his own, and aware early on of the enriching value of a broad general culture. These diplomas would stand him in good stead with his family (always fearful that the musical avenue would turn into a dead-end street), and they would smooth his integration into those layers of society in which the arts were but one of the subjects of fashionable, and intellectual, conversation.

Cherubini's Conservatoire

Berlioz's initiation into love came at an early age, his initiation into big-city life when he was just eighteen, his initiation into the professional world of music in his early twenties. (Many composers proceeded in the opposite order.) It was during the period of his medical studies that Berlioz learned the true art of musical composition, essentially by going to the opera, by absorbing the ingredients of the craft with uncommon recall, and by adopting the time-honored technique of copying out the works of the masters. We know that he heard Salieri's *Les Danaïdes*, Méhul's *Stratonice*, Spontini's *La Vestale* and *Fernand Cortez*, and Gluck's *Iphigénie en Aulide* and *Iphigénie en Tauride*. The *Mémoires* would have us believe that it was after a performance of the latter, on 21 November 1821, that Berlioz swore to himself that he would become a composer. This may be, although the scientific examination that he passed in January 1824 argues against taking the oath as literal truth. Even after the successful performance of his *Messe solennelle*, in July 1825, his teacher exclaimed that "you will be neither a doctor nor an apothecary but a great composer" – something he would not have said, I think, had thoughts of a medical career been totally abandoned so many years before.

Berlioz did copy out passages from Gluck's *Iphigénie* operas in 1822, and he made a calligraphic copy of *Tauride* in April of 1824. A note he made in this manuscript speaks volumes about his musical sensibilities at the time, and about his attitude toward the larger musical public. Six bars before the end of Iphigénie's air at the opening of Act III, "D'une image, hélas! trop chérie," in which she laments her long lost brother Orestes, Gluck writes an unusually piquant harmony to underscore the words "sombres bords" – for she feels that only "beyond the grave" will she ever see her brother again. Next to the strange E natural in the bass, Berlioz writes: "If someone capable of understanding the slightest thing about music is not totally overcome with nervous excitement at this E natural in the bass, then he is quite obviously deprived of any sensitivity whatsoever to dramatic music." The surprise created by the E natural, which abuts an E flat in the preceding bar, may be a subtle one, but at the time it was shocking enough. What is noteworthy is the way Berlioz expresses his enthusiasm, in a comment (addressed to whom?) that would reprimand those who might miss Gluck's moving musical illustration.[4]

Berlioz was twenty-one at the time, he had been a private pupil of Jean-François Lesueur's for over a year (having entered into the good graces of the highly regarded composer by showing him *Le Cheval arabe*, a cantata for voice and orchestra, now lost), he had determined definitively to pursue music, and he was confident of his success. He wrote to his father on 31 August 1824 that he was "involuntarily" drawn not to his downfall, but to a "magnificent career":

I believe and I am convinced that I will distinguish myself in music; all external circumstances lead me to believe it, and internally the voice of nature is far more powerful than the most rigorous voices of reason. I would have every imaginable chance for success should you wish to support me. [. . .] In the final analysis I want to make a name for myself, I want to leave upon this earth a few traces of my existence. And so great is the depth of this desire, which is nothing if not noble, that I should prefer to be Gluck or Méhul dead than to be what I am now in the fullness of life.

It is from correspondence such as this that we learn that Berlioz was easily able and unembarrassed to study himself, to share his feelings, and forcefully to articulate his innermost thoughts. Berlioz's public speech was not always in accord with his private thought (something that suggests he was human), but there is ample evidence in his letters of his deep devotion to family and friends, and of his inclination to assurance and enthusiasm as opposed to sadness and suffering (which came, towards the end, to dominate his outward emotional stance). Over three thousand five hundred of his letters have been preserved, and it is likely that he wrote far more than twice that number. The best of these transmit information and disclose emotion with an evident love of language and an unusually incisive calligraphy that bespeaks the man's lifelong passion for the exact.

Berlioz would often speak of Gluck as his first musical hero, as he does in the passage quoted here; in later years he would be closely associated with the revivals of *Orphée* at the Théâtre Lyrique, in 1859, and *Alceste*, at the Opéra, in 1861 and 1866. He was also imbued early on with the works of Spontini and Lesueur (who was Napoleon's chapelmaster before taking on that position for the restored Bourbon kings). These composers represented not only styles but worlds of music associated with the *ancien régime*, the turbulence of the Revolution, and the rhetoric of the First Empire. Most of us know their works inadequately, and find it curious that their essentially classic comportment could have provoked in Berlioz his "fatal attraction" to musical composition. A more likely *provocateur* was Beethoven, who did indeed become an essential model for Berlioz, but only after the foundation of the Conservatoire Orchestra, the Société des Concerts, in 1828 – when the symphonies were performed with a flawlessness and fire that kindled the imaginations of all who heard them. By that time Berlioz had no lingering doubts about his chosen profession, and was only further inspired by the precision and power of this soon-to-be world-renowned ensemble.

Berlioz first came to the École royale de musique on the eve of Luigi Cherubini's ascendancy to the directorship. (The name "Conservatoire" reminded the Bourbons of the institution's revolutionary origins and was suppressed until 1831.) Several able associates of Louis XVIII had managed to have this naturalized Frenchman named chief administrator of the school, and he assumed the leadership in April 1822. Cherubini was then in the late summer of his career as the composer of more than two dozen Italian and French operas, and the composer whom Beethoven considered the equal of Haydn and Mozart. He would now devote body and soul to improving the education offered by the premier music school in France, doing loyal battle – for increased financial support, new faculty positions, renovations to the building, and modern equipment – with many of the dignitaries and functionaries of the régime of Charles X. Thousands of letters preserved in the archives prove that every decision, from the acceptance of the budgets (when they were reasonable) to the expulsion of the students (when they were not), was made by Cherubini in consultation with the uncommonly wealthy and powerful director of the department of fine arts for the governments of the restored Bourbon kings, the Vicomte Sosthènes de La Rochefoucauld (see illustration 2). And they suggest, as do the reminiscences of Berlioz and others, that tolerance and affability were not the chief characteristics of Cherubini's law-and-order personality.

Among the new director's first reforms was the reduction of the number of students, especially in the piano department, in order to separate the wheat from the chaff. Since the mid-teens, pianists had

2 Sosthènes de La Rochefoucauld, Director of Fine Arts (1824–1830), one of Berlioz's first "official" protectors. (Drawing by Mlle Th. Sandrié, *ca.* 1825.)

been arriving in Paris and seeking conservatory training in over-whelming numbers, something that was seen as increasingly at odds with the institution's patriotic purpose of furnishing the nation with native musicians. This is the reason that foreign pianists now became ineligible to enroll – the reason for Cherubini's legendary refusal to admit even that young phenomenon, Franz Liszt, for example, who had the misfortune of being Hungarian, not French. (The Belgian César Franck was admitted to the school only after his father became a French citizen.) Cherubini would soon undertake to raise the level of vocal instruction, too, much prompted by the Vicomte de La Rochefoucauld, who was himself spurred on by Rossini. Accordingly, three Italians were appointed to the voice department in 1827, among them Davidde Banderali (whose private students included Marie Récio, Berlioz's eventual mistress and second wife, and whose daughter would become one of Marie's closest friends).

When Berlioz began to frequent the Conservatoire, shortly after his arrival in Paris in 1821, it was thus in a period of reorganization. But the library of the school (along with instrument collection, which was composed of items confiscated from aristocratic émigrés and from those elsewhere conquered by Napoleon) was already considered unique in Europe. It was here that Berlioz came to study the scores of the masters, and it was here that he had a first, tragi-comical encounter with Cherubini. In an effort to enforce the puritanical principles on which the relations between the sexes at the school were based, Cherubini had decreed that men and women were to use separate doors at opposite ends of the building. (A copy of the decree is found in the archives.) Knowing nothing of this moral edict, Berlioz unwittingly entered by the *female* door, at which point an obsequious custodian reported him to the new director for having done so. In one of those priceless vignettes that characterize his *Mémoires*, Berlioz relates the skirmish that ensued. Fiercely interrogated by the cadaverous director, Berlioz (aware of the law of 3 August 1795 that rendered the school unrestricted) replied coolly that he needed no one's permission to use the facility:

> "The Conservatoire library is open to the public from ten till three and I have the right to use it."
> "The – the – the right?"

"Yes, sir."

"I weell not allow you to return."

"I shall return none the less."

"What – what – what ees your name?" he yelled, shaking with rage.

"Sir," I answered, growing pale in my turn, "my name will perhaps be familiar to you one day – but you shall not have it now."

"S-s-seize 'eem, Hottin," he cried to the porter, "I'll 'ave 'eem in preeson."

Thereupon, to the stupefaction of the onlookers, two of them, master and servant, began pursuing me round the table, knocking over stools and reading-desks in a vain attempt to catch me. In the end I made my escape, calling out with a laugh as I fled, "You shan't have me or my name, and I shall soon be back again to study Gluck's scores."

David Cairns's translation captures Berlioz's imitation of Cherubini's Italian accent, which apparently lent an air of ridicule to this otherwise highly authoritarian figure. The young man's impertinence was hardly sagacious in a musical world in which the senior Italian composer wielded considerable influence, and whatever our reaction may be ex post facto, Cherubini was not amused. Indeed, Berlioz's portrait of Cherubini remained a source of anguish even to his grand-daughter, more than a decade after our composer's death, when she attempted to insert a corrective letter into the second printing of Berlioz's *Mémoires*.[5] (That Berlioz had a high regard for Cherubini's music is something that history has swept under the rug.)

Copying scores in the library and tutoring with Lesueur were essential to Berlioz's musical education, but the decisive act came only later, on 26 August 1826, when he actually enrolled in Lesueur's course in composition at the Conservatoire, and on 2 October 1826, when he signed up for Antonin Reicha's course in counterpoint and fugue. These inscriptions appear in an archival register in the inimitably shaky hand of Cherubini himself, who apparently admitted the now almost twenty-three-year-old Berlioz on an exceptional basis, since the normal age limit for these classes was twenty.[6] The school year ran from the beginning of October to the end of August, and classes normally met once a week for two hours. But Lesueur was permitted to give his lessons at home, where they often extended well beyond the normal two-hour period. Berlioz appears to have remained with Lesueur at the Conservatoire for four years, and with Reicha for two. He was removed from the school's registers on 25 August 1830, at the time of his victory in the competition for the Prix de Rome.

By the time of his matriculation, in 1826, Berlioz had already composed a good deal of music, of which most is now lost. Of the two operas *Estelle et Némorin* and *Les Francs-Juges*, the oratorio *Le Passage de la mer rouge*, the two dramatic scenes, *Beverley, ou le joueur* and *La Révolution grecque*, only the last, along with fragments of *Les Francs-Juges*, have been preserved. A Latin *Messe solennelle*, commissioned by the chapelmaster at the Église Saint-Roch in Paris for performance in the autumn of 1824, was long presumed lost as well, for Berlioz tells us that after performing the work, in 1825 and 1827, he burnt the score. However, to the astonishment of Berliozians everywhere, the four-hundred page autograph of this Mass was discovered by chance, in Antwerp, in 1991. From it we learn that parts of later fully formed works such as the *Symphonie fantastique* (1830), the *Requiem* (1837), the opera *Benvenuto Cellini* (1838), and the *Te Deum* (1849) derive in significant ways from a sacred work composed in Berlioz's early days as a student!

The 1824 performance did not come off: the very first rehearsal was a catastrophe because the inexperienced composer had failed to prepare the parts with sufficient care. To cover the expenses of a later performance, he boldly asked the celebrated writer and statesman François-René de Chateaubriand for a loan of twelve hundred francs. But Chateaubriand was unable to oblige. (Berlioz would print his sincere letter of regret in the *Mémoires*.) The performance of the Mass that did take place – on 10 July 1825, the first time a major work by Berlioz was heard in public – was in fact made possible by a loan from another aristocratic friend, Augustin de Pons. A second performance took place in November 1827, after which, except as a source for an extraordinary series of self-borrowings, the music was abandoned. Newly rediscovered, the Mass has now been published, performed, and recorded. Apart from its intrinsic merits, it stands as a living reminder of the difficulty of distinguishing "early" Berlioz from "late," for style, always precarious as evidence, is in his case particularly difficult to interpret.

Also in Berlioz's portfolio at the time of his entrance into the Conservatoire was the score of an opera on which he had been working intermittently, after 1825, with a young law student who had become and would forever remain one of his closest friends. Jean-Jacques-Humbert Ferrand was born in 1805 in Belley, a town about fifty kilometers northeast of Berlioz's home at La Côte-Saint-André, and went to Paris, like so many upwardly mobile men from the country, to pursue his father's profession (the law) while exercising with some assiduousness, as he would throughout his life, his literary avocation. In Berlioz's *Mémoires*, Ferrand is evoked with especial warmth:

> You have often stood by me in the heat of the struggle and fortified
> me in times of despondency, and given me heart for future ordeals by
> recalling the victories of the past; to you with your keen and lofty
> feeling for beauty, your religious respect for the truth and your belief
> in the power and greatness of art, the tale of my explorations,
> discoveries, and experiences in Europe will not, I trust, prove without
> interest. No patronage I might win could be more sympathetic or
> discerning than yours.

In addition to preparing the libretto of *Les Francs-Juges*, the three-act tale whose title may be rendered as "The Vehmic Judges" or "The Judges of the Secret Court," Ferrand mused with Berlioz over other works, lent him money, and wrote to him intimately and faithfully for some forty years. While Ferrand's letters to the composer no longer exist, Berlioz's to Ferrand do. Indeed, they were published in 1882 under the appropriate title of *Hector Berlioz – Lettres intimes*, and have long been a principal source of biographical information. Letter-writing was always a regular part of the workday for Berlioz, as it was for Chateaubriand, Musset, Stendhal, Balzac, Flaubert, Baudelaire, Sand, Gautier and so many others of the time. For all of them it surely had the therapeutic effect of heart-to-heart conversation that it had for Berlioz: writing to his sister in 1858, he said that "when I chat with you in this way, it seems to me that I am breathing an air that is fresh, and restorative." He might have said the same to Ferrand.

The passage above shows why Berlioz shared his most profound aspirations and intimate thoughts with this minor littérateur, devout Catholic, and supporter of the old Bourbon monarchy. Like another orthodox Catholic friend, the journalist and musicographer Joseph d'Ortigue, Ferrand believed with Berlioz, apart from any question of the existence of the deity (about which Berlioz was skeptical), that an artist was morally accountable to the goddess of Art.

From the several fragments of Les Francs-Juges that have been preserved, D. Kern Holoman has deftly reconstructed the opera, with its evil rulers and innocent maids suggestive of the Germanic folk-story manner of Weber's Der Freischütz, and he has shown where sections of the work found homes in Berlioz's more mature compositions – for here, too, a work eventually abandoned was mined by the composer for treasure used later. The march that is well known as the fourth movement of the Symphonie fantastique, for example, was originally the penultimate number of the opera's second act.

It is therefore clear that the Berlioz who entered the Conservatoire in the autumn of 1826 did so not as a neophyte seeking basic instruction, but as a well-prepared young musician, tutored and self-taught, seeking experience, refinement, and a passport to a professional career. This required further training in the skills of harmony and counterpoint. It also required, or so one might suppose, training in accompaniment, or figured bass, or in what we would call "secondary piano": Berlioz's friend Ferdinand Hiller certainly thought that the piano was essential to any musician's education, and many since have tried to account for the uniqueness of Berlioz's music as a result of his failure to learn to play that instrument. That his family at La Côte had not wished to invest in such an expensive item is understandable; but it is indeed curious that Berlioz did not make time during his student days in Paris to develop more than a primitive facility at the keyboard – doubly curious in that the instrument was in an active state of mechanical development, something which, as we know from later reports, Berlioz always followed with interest. Berlioz did play the flute and the guitar, as we have seen, and he sang well enough to avoid embarrassment in public. But a pianist, despite everything, he was destined not to become.

Above and beyond enrollment at the Conservatoire, the decision to become a composer required, in all but name, competing for the Prix de Rome. By the time he finally won the prize, in the summer of 1830, Berlioz had given several important concerts designed, I think more than anything else, to give him leverage. If he already had a public following, he believed, the judges could not easily deny him the prize that would signal his entry into the world of the professional composer – into the world, that is, to which compositional training at the Conservatoire was geared: that of the stage of the Parisian operatic theater.

Paying (for) concerts

Berlioz was hardly destined to be a church musician, notwithstanding the importance to his career of the *Messe solennelle* of the mid-eighteen-twenties. And despite the youthful operatic enthusiasms of *Les Francs-Juges* and *Richard en Palestine* (an opéra comique he envisaged in 1826 and 1827 but did not pursue), he soon learned that performance at the Opéra or Opéra Comique required the "pull" and prestige of the Prix de Rome. In addition to doing battle in the traditional arena of the annual prize competition, which we shall visit below, he thus opened a second front, attempting to gain a following by giving public concerts of his own.

Concert life was little developed in the Paris of the restored

Bourbon kings, Louis XVI's brothers Louis XVIII and Charles X, who were particularly beneficent towards the spoken drama, opening certain theaters that Napoleon had closed, and appearing frequently in the house. The lyric theater, too, became a royal preoccupation, for the regeneration of the Paris Opéra that began in the later eighteen-twenties – and that culminated in momentous performances of Auber's *La Muette de Portici*, Rossini's *Guillaume Tell*, and Meyerbeer's *Robert le diable* – was a phenomenon of the Restoration, and not of the July Monarchy (despite the 1831 première of the last-mentioned work). Instrumental in establishing the pre-eminence of the spectacular form that we now know as French Grand Opera was the Vicomte de La Rochefoucauld, whose approval and assistance had been required every step of the way.

It was the Vicomte, too, who facilitated the foundation of the Société des Concerts du Conservatoire, which for the first time in France brought symphonic music to the fore at the highest professional level. Unlike other European orchestras, which depended for their existence upon traditional aristocratic patronage, here was one that was instigated as a cooperative venture by its founder and long-time first conductor, François-Antoine Habeneck, and that was supported to varying degrees over the years by the state. It was the Vicomte, therefore, to whom Berlioz had to appeal when he determined, in the spring of 1828, to put on a concert of his own in the only proper space for the performance of large-scale instrumental music, the concert hall at the Conservatoire.

Not without objection from Cherubini, Berlioz did manage to obtain *la vieille salle*, as the auditorium was known to generations of musicians in the nineteenth century, and to give, on 26 May 1828, the first of many hundreds of concerts for which he was impresario, contractor, director of publicity, artistic adviser and, last but not least, the principal if not the sole composer represented on the program. On this occasion – rather like Beethoven's first public concert in Vienna, which symbolized his emergence upon the scene as a figure of exceptional creativity – the featured works were the just-completed *Waverley*

Overture (Berlioz's "Opus 1," with a title from Sir Walter Scott and a dedication to his uncle Félix Marmion), the Scène héroïque (with a text by Ferrand on the current struggle for independence in Greece, in its first and only performance), excerpts from the Messe solennelle, and selections from Les Francs-Juges.

In fact the Grande Ouverture des Francs-Juges, given here, came to be performed on some sixty occasions during Berlioz's lifetime – more even than witnessed by the most brilliant of his concert overtures, Le Carnaval romain of 1844. The Francs-Juges Overture is the work that first introduced the composer to audiences in many of the German towns, and later, to audiences in Boston and New York. The piece shares some of the fire and brimstone of Beethoven's Overture to Egmont – the key of F minor, for example, and the prototypically dramatic progression from darkness to light – which may account for its subsequent acceptance and popularity. One wonders if Berlioz took something of his F minor agitation from the overture to Cherubini's opera of 1797, Médée, from which Beethoven, also, learned a thing or two. But for the lumbering tune associated with his opera's chief villain, Berlioz liberates the brass (four horns, three trumpets, three trombones, two ophicleides) in an uninhibited manner that is common to neither earlier composer.

The expenses of the concert of 26 May 1828 exceeded the profits, and loans from family and friends had to make up the difference. But the press was largely favorable: Berlioz had made a "début that will lead somewhere," as Fétis put it in the one Parisian magazine uniquely devoted to music, the Revue musicale, and he had made a splash.

But the impact failed to win over all the judges in the summer Prix de Rome competitions of either 1828 or 1829. Accordingly, on 1 November 1829, in the same hard-won hall at the Conservatoire – Cherubini always felt that concerts "foreign" to the establishment "disturbed the normal schedule of rehearsals and interrupted the daily classes"[7] – Berlioz undertook to present a more ambitious program that included the overtures to Les Francs-Juges and Waverley, Le Jugement dernier (extracted from the Messe solennelle), the Concert des *sylphes* from the recently completed *Huit Scènes de Faust* (Berlioz's immediate reaction to his first reading of Goethe's drama, later transformed into *La Damnation de Faust*), and Beethoven's *Emperor* Concerto, with Ferdinand Hiller as soloist. This time, in order to reduce expenses, Berlioz asked for exemption from the normal license fee that concert-givers had to pay to the Opéra (which kept its coffers full by exacting taxes on all other music-giving venues) and for a reduction of the poor tax – normally, twenty-five percent of the gross receipts – which was always assessed upon entrepreneurs in the arts to support the good works of the public hospitals (where patients were treated free of charge). Rather than a percentage of the gate, Berlioz proposed a flat payment of sixty francs.[8] His request received the approval of the various persons who had authority over the matter, largely because they understood that to make his works known Berlioz would have to distribute a large number of complimentary tickets, and because they assumed that sixty francs would in any case be roughly equal to a quarter of the receipts.

The *droit des pauvres* or poor tax was something against which Berlioz frequently railed, troubled as he was by the notion that artists, supported by a fortunate few, should somehow buoy up those down-trodden members of society who were unable to afford the luxury of music and the theater. Berlioz and others regularly applied for exceptions to this sometimes confiscatory tax, and their efforts – suggesting fixed sums in place of a fixed percentage of the receipts – occasionally met with success. When the Revolution of 1848 broke out, Berlioz immediately expressed the hope that at least the hated poor tax would now be abolished, so much did it weigh on his mind. In fact it endured in one form or another until the nineteen-seventies, when it was finally subsumed under the modern value-added tax.

The total receipts from the concert came to five hundred and twenty-eight francs and, after paying all the bills, Berlioz was left with one hundred and fifty francs – a not insignificant sum that would more than double his monthly income.

In gratitude for genuine assistance in 1828 and 1829, when Berlioz initiated these first large-scale concerts, the composer took the extraordinary step of dedicating Huit Scènes de Faust to the Vicomte de La Rochefoucauld, who accepted the dedication on 17 March 1829 with an acknowledgment of Berlioz's "eminently worthy" talents as he took the first steps in his career. The dedication itself, which some have regarded as politically motivated, was in fact a sincere and unreserved step in the right direction, for it showed that Berlioz, who could be consumed by Art and by Love, was capable of dealing with the practical realities of a world rarely so finely tuned to the arts as he. Indeed, when he earlier invited the Vicomte to his concert of 26 May 1828, he wrote to the director of fine arts, with some urgency (on 24 May 1828), that "it is your approbation that I most fervently desire, for the fate of artists in general and that of composers in particular depends upon you and you alone":

> Without you I would never have been able to overcome the obstacles that have been placed in my way on all sides. Indeed, it is very difficult for me to describe the gratitude that I feel. May I someday be able to prove to you that I was not unworthy of the protection you have offered! This is my most ardent and heartfelt wish.

The tone of this communication is rather more personal than that of the normal business letter, even though the writer was a mere student, and the recipient was a man whose father, the Duc de Doudeauville, was Minister of the Royal Household and a member of the King's confidential inner circle. I take this as a sign that Berlioz recognized and appreciated what must have been the Vicomte's essentially compassionate nature. Sosthènes de La Rochefoucauld was much ridiculed at the time for being so straight-laced as to have had the sensitive parts of public statues covered with fig-leaves, and the sensitive parts of ballerinas covered with long skirts in an excess of what was literally a case of politically correct behavior. But this sort of prudishness ought not forever to diminish our estimation of his character. Beyond overruling Cherubini and acting firmly on Berlioz's behalf, the Vicomte had been a highly effective advocate for musical enterprises, as I have already suggested, and during his tenure he managed to double the credits allotted by the government to the arts. It is in a way unfortunate that he had no choice but to resign in the aftermath of the Revolution of 1830 (like other aristocrats, he was allergic to the Orléans branch of the royal family), for it is my sense that had he been able or inclined to remain, Berlioz would have benefited from having in command this particular official who, despite his reputation, was not without warmth. In 1837 George Sand, a close friend, reassured him of her high regard for his goodwill and generosity, saying "I know that you have the warmest heart and most noble character that anyone could possibly encounter."9 By suggesting that the man actually had a sense of humor, as he does in chapter 18 of the *Mémoires*, Berlioz, too, lends fullness to the Vicomte's otherwise far too austere reputation.

If the concerts of 1828 and 1829 were designed to force the hand of the judges when the time came to hear the prize cantatas in the summer months, so, too, was the concert that Berlioz hoped to put on in the spring of 1830, when he had in hand the freshly completed draft of the *Symphonie fantastique*. Even earlier, after two of the nine *Mélodies irlandaises* he composed in 1829 were sung at a concert in February of the new year, he felt, as he wrote to his father, that he had begun to have

> everything necessary to establish an outstanding reputation:
> passionate advocates and furious adversaries who argue whether I
> am losing my mind and am half-crazed or whether I am an evil genius
> come to *destroy* and not to enlighten. My innovations simply leave
> them beside themselves.

For various reasons, the performance projected for the spring had to be put off until the fall. Meanwhile, in July, the three-day Revolution toppled the throne of Charles X and established Louis-Philippe as King of the French. In August, Berlioz was awarded the Grand Prix de Rome.

The paradoxical Prix de Rome

"Monsieur Berlioz, one of the most distinguished artists in Paris, to whom we are obliged for several articles on music that have appeared in our journal, has just won the First Grand Prize at the Royal Conservatory of Music" – so wrote a columnist for Le Rénovateur on 27 August 1830. The Prix de Rome for musicians was instituted in 1803, and during the first hundred years of its existence, only a handful of winners became figures of wide renown, among them Ferdinand Hérold (1812), Fromental Halévy (1818), Ambroise Thomas (1832), Charles Gounod (1839), Georges Bizet (1857), Jules Massenet (1867), Claude Debussy (1884), and Gustave Charpentier (1889). An equal number of celebrated composers failed to win the prize, among them Félicien David, César Franck, Édouard Lalo, Emmanuel Chabrier, Camille Saint-Saëns, Vincent d'Indy, Léo Délibes, and most famously (because his non-victory created a scandal), Maurice Ravel. This does give pause for thought regarding the efficacy of the competition, but the finger of blame, if blame one wishes to attribute, is often pointed at the wrong institution, for the prize is often misunderstood – as it was by the editors of Le Rénovateur in 1830 – as being offered by the Conservatoire itself.

In fact it was offered by the Académie des Beaux-Arts of the Institut de France in an annual concours open to French citizens of a certain age who did not have to be, though they invariably were, students at the Conservatoire. Indeed, Berlioz himself was not officially enrolled at the school, in the summer of 1826, when he first entered the competition. Then, as always, the eliminatory first round began with an academic exercise in counterpoint, on a given subject, which was judged by the members of the music section of the Academy (who were naturally partial to their own students at the school on the other side of the Seine). Immediately after his failed attempt at the preliminary competition in 1826 – the fugue he wrote is of certifiably poor quality, as Julian Rushton has adroitly demonstrated – Berlioz may have felt a genuine need for further technical instruction. He certainly knew that his chances for success would be greater if courses at the

Conservatoire were on his curriculum vitae. He may have been less conscious of the wisdom of befriending the director. Cherubini was a musical guru to generations of government functionaries assigned to the arts: if he had become Berlioz's musical godfather, little would have slowed the young man's early musical momentum.

Those who did survive the preliminary competition went on to the main event, the composition of a cantata for solo voice (or voices) and orchestra on a prescribed text, usually one of classical subject-matter and formality. (The masters had devised the competition in this way, as an exercise in dramatic vocal music rather than in string-quartet writing, for example, which one would imagine a hypothetical Viennese academy might have designed, since opera was the sole category from which a composer in France could make a living by *composing*.) The members of the music section were joined by the other luminaries of the Academy (the painters, sculptors, architects, and engravers) for the adjudication of the winner of the grand prize, and that fortunate fellow – no woman took top honors until the dawn of the twentieth century – received a five-year government fellowship to spend two years in Rome, one year in Germany, and two years back in Paris establishing himself in the artistic community.

After completing the preliminary round in 1827 (this time his fugue was sound), Berlioz wrote a cantata entitled *La Mort d'Orphée* that went unrewarded largely because its innovative orchestral textures were nearly impossible to reproduce on the piano (which instrument served the singers when the judges made their decisions). His *Herminie*, of 1828 (Pierre-Ange Vieillard's text derived from Tasso's *Jerusalem Delivered*, and tells of the heretical Erminia's love for the Christian hero Tancred), was found more promising – the concert of 26 May 1828 had served a purpose – and it was awarded a second prize that carried with it free *entrées* to the principal theaters of the capital (a valuable commodity in Paris, where theater tickets were dear), exemption from further examination at the Conservatoire (whose registers now list him as "2d prix"), exemption from military service, and, most importantly, the unofficial guarantee of a first prize in the following year.

With this in mind, after the competition of 1828, Berlioz made a rather daring effort to secure a government stipend for his work as a composer. On 20 August, with a note from Lesueur testifying to his talent and promise of success, he wrote to the Minister of the Interior, the Comte de Martignac, to ask for an annual *encouragement*. During the Restoration and the July Monarchy certain men and women of distinction did indeed receive government allowances of this sort, simply in their capacity as artists, although the evidence suggests that their political views were not foreign to those who offered the cash. Berlioz's friend, the Baron Taylor (who would years later be one of the pall-bearers at the composer's funeral), was awarded an annual *pension littéraire*, for example, as a man "no less distinguished by artistic talent than by his monarchical sentiments."[10] In June 1830, the Ministry of the Interior was giving annual *encouragements* to, among others, Prosper Mérimée (900 francs), Alphonse de Lamartine (1,500 francs), Charles Nodier (1,500 francs), and Victor Hugo (2,000 francs). (Such payments – whose amounts might be regarded as contemporary measures of talent – continued to be made under Louis-Philippe on an ad hoc basis, always, apparently, by special request.) In January 1831, for example, the composer François-Adrien Boieldieu received a one-time payment of twelve hundred francs, and the widow of the composer Étienne-Nicolas Méhul received a payment of one thousand francs.[11] Berlioz's effort to obtain funding in 1828 was unsuccessful, but later, he, too, would occasionally partake of moneys set aside by the government for the encouragement of the arts.

Despite the "guarantee" implicit in the second prize in 1828 (or perhaps because of it), Berlioz's *Cléopâtre*, of 1829, so surprised the judges with its unorthodox harmonies and unconventional melodies that they failed to follow tradition, reneged on their "promise," and awarded no prize at all. (The text was again by Vieillard, whose name means "old man." One can well imagine the buffoonery, sophomoric and other, that this produced among Berlioz and his chums.)

On 14 July 1830, for the fifth time since 1826, Berlioz completed the exercises of the preliminary competition at the Institute. With his fugue deemed satisfactory, he entered *en loge* on the 17th and emerged, twelve days later, to join the fighting in the streets: revolution in Paris had broken out on 27 July, ignited primarily by King Charles X's edict, published on the 26th, that suspended freedom of the press and thus abrogated one of the fundamental freedoms guaranteed by the Constitutional Charter of 1814. Workers, students, and defectors from the National Guard raided the armories, barricaded the streets, set tri-colored flags atop Notre Dame and the Hôtel de Ville, and put Paris into a state of siege. In only three days the fate of the embattled old monarch was sealed. The Duc d'Orléans, called to take the throne by the leaders of the provisional government, became Roi des Français – King of the French – on 9 August 1830.

During what has become known as *Les Trois Glorieuses*, Berlioz had a front-row seat. Tempted immediately to join the fighting in the streets, he none the less had the presence of mind to complete the score of his cantata. "Only the desperate importance of this competition was able to keep me inside our barricaded and thickly walled fortress," he told his father on 2 August. He sincerely regretted not having been able to join his efforts to those who had "paid with their blood for the purchase of our liberties." The events were still fresh in his mind when he came to describe the events in his *Mémoires*:

> I shall never forget how Paris looked during those famous days: the frantic bravery of the street urchins, the enthusiasm of the men, the wild excitement of the whores, the grim resignation of the Swiss and Royal Guards, the curious pride of the workers in having mastered the city, as they said, yet having plundered nothing, and the astounding braggadocio of some of the young people who, having demonstrated genuine courage, found a way of rendering it ridiculous by the manner in which they recounted their exploits, adding grotesque embellishments to the truth.

In July of 1830 Berlioz was moved, not troubled, by the pomposity of the gladiators. And in a verse he later wrote for the work that commemorated the tenth anniversary of the July Revolution, the *Symphonie funèbre et triomphale*, he yet again mentioned the blood that they had shed for Liberty, "l'honneur de la patrie."

The revolution delayed the adjudication of the prizes until the latter part of August. On the 19th, for the members of the music section, and on the 21st, for the members of the Academy as a whole, Alexis Dupont sang Berlioz's cantata, *Sardanapale*, with piano accompaniment. It was judged the best of the lot and awarded the First Grand Prize. Two days later Berlioz wrote to his mother: "It is at long last my great pleasure to announce to you that I have won the celebrated prize. It is mine." "Ce *fameux* prix" is how he put it – the adjective means famous and infamous simultaneously, and Berlioz intended both. He was delighted to win, but claimed that in order to do so he had had to write what he regarded as an undistinguished work. He always found it abhorrent that a group of obstinate conventionalists should sit in judgment of aspiring innovators, and he made this idea one of the *idées fixes* of his writings. (Richard Wagner, too, wrote a musical variation on this theme; it is encapsulated in *Die Meistersinger von Nürnberg*.)

Sardanapale is based on the story of the decadent Assyrian king whose death is immortalized in what may be Eugène Delacroix's greatest tableau, *La Mort de Sardanapale*. Only a fragment of Berlioz's cantata survives (the last of its five sections: *Cavatine*, *Bacchanale*, *Air héroïque*, *Air final*, *Incendie*), and this is unfortunate, for I think he slyly exaggerated its mediocrity as a way of condemning the old fogies of the Academy whose judgment he had made it a principle to detest. I will not be surprised if some day the complete manuscript turns up, for despite the fact that Berlioz tells us he burnt it, the official copy that had to be deposited at the secretariat of the Institute should have found its way to the library, and not to Berlioz's fiery stove.

Berlioz was duly crowned at a ceremony that took place on 30 October 1830. Many have quoted the *Mémoires'* hilarious description of the prize-giving ritual without realizing that it is more than a spoof of what took place at the Institute, for a *distribution des prix* occurred every year at nearly every educational institution in France, and these were

3   *La Mort de Sardanapale*, painted by Delacroix between 1827 and 1828. Berlioz
won the Prix de Rome in 1830 with a cantata on the same subject.

regularly illustrated and repeatedly mocked for the kind of strict
adherence to tradition that Berlioz satirizes in his own chapter 30:

> The laureate rises. He embraces the Permanent Secretary [the official
> in charge]. There is polite applause. A few feet from the Permanent
> Secretary's rostrum sits the laureate's illustrious master. The
> laureate embraces his illustrious master. This is only natural. There
> is more polite applause. On a bench at the back, behind the
> academicians, the laureate's parents shed silent tears of joy. The
> laureate vaults over the intervening benches (treading on one
> person's toe, tramping on another person's coat) and flings himself
> into the arms of his father and mother, who by now are sobbing
> unashamedly. This is only natural. But there is no more polite
> applause. People are beginning to laugh.

In fact Berlioz himself was in no mood for laughter on the
appointed day, for neither his parents nor his illustrious master were

in attendance. More important, the *Incendie* that he had added specifically for this public performance – his musical "explosion," as he called it – simply failed to ignite. The players missed a series of cues because the horns failed to come in at the appointed time. "Five hundred thousand curses on all musicians who fail to count their rests!!!" Berlioz exclaimed, and he hurled his score into the middle of the orchestra. (There is indirect confirmation of this outburst in some of the press reports on the event.) But the prize he sought was no less won.

Of the four cantatas Berlioz wrote for the Prix de Rome, only this one came to performance during Berlioz's lifetime – here at the Institute, on 30 October 1830, one month later at the Conservatoire, on 5 December 1830 (when the principal attraction on the program was the première of the *Symphonie fantastique*), and on two later occasions in 1833 and 1834. Along with *La Mort d'Orphée, Herminie,* and *Cléopâtre, Sardanapale* was then put into a musical savings account from which the composer made regular withdrawals over the next several decades. Parts of *Orphée* and *Cléopâtre* found their way into *Lélio ou le Retour à la vie* and *Benvenuto Cellini;* the opening theme of *Herminie,* modified, became the *idée fixe* of the *Fantastique;* and passages from *Sardanapale* made their way into the scores of *Roméo et Juliette, L'Impériale,* and *Les Troyens.*

In 1830 Berlioz had a lot riding on the prize. Victory necessitated a sojourn in Italy (Berlioz had misgivings about this, but the Italian experience would impregnate his creative imagination for years to come), it meant a three-thousand-franc stipend (which immediately became the chief source of his income – three thousand francs was the typical annual salary, for example, of a first-desk player in the orchestra at the Conservatoire), and it demonstrated to his still doubtful family that his career was legitimate, his talent genuine, his prospects excellent. Indeed, his teacher, deeply proud of Berlioz's accomplishment, felt that the prize marked the beginning of what would be a long and glorious career. In a remarkable letter to Berlioz's father written four days after the Academy had determined the winner, the seventy-year-old Lesueur, who had been the official composer of the Napoleonic Empire and who now dreamed that Berlioz might become "the Napoleon of musical science," went immediately to the heart of the matter that most concerned the hard-working country doctor: your son has won the First Grand Prize, Lesueur told him; "he is to receive a stipend for the next five years." Reserving his congratulations for later, Lesueur painted a picture based on considerable personal experience:

> Handel died a very rich man; Gluck's income at the end was 50,000 francs; Grétry's 30,000; I knew Paisiello intimately when he was enjoying an income of 40,000 francs from pensions he received from all the courts of Europe, and from the annuities that he had established; Rossini now possesses a very large fortune; Méhul, who benefited from a generous pension, lived in comfort throughout his entire life; Haydn had only a moderate income, it is true, but like many other great composers, he established a European-wide reputation. Your son will do likewise.

Lesueur went on to predict celebrity for the Berlioz family name and to express satisfaction at having supported Berlioz's defection from medicine to music:

> I dare say that your son's reputation will rise to the highest level that is possible for a great composer, and that he will become the beneficiary of honor, respect, and an illustrious name. With all of that one cannot fail to procure, if not a very great fortune (which is always a matter of chance), at least a respectable livelihood.

Also riding on the prize in 1830 was Berlioz's credibility in the eyes of the parents of the young woman with whom he had been desperately in love for some four months, Marie Moke (known as Camille), for they, too, required that Berlioz secure at least a "respectable livelihood" in order to present himself as a suitable match for their musically gifted daughter.

It was probably while giving guitar lessons at a school for girls in the Marais, at the beginning of 1830, that Berlioz met the darkly beautiful Camille, then a piano instructor at the same institution. She was Ferdinand Hiller's girlfriend at the time, but she became fascinated with Berlioz, perhaps because he recounted to her his terrible obsession with Harriet Smithson (whom we will meet below), which he had suffered ever since seeing the Irish actress on the stage in the autumn of 1827. Camille seems to have reported to Berlioz certain "horrible truths" about Miss Smithson – to console her new-found friend? to foster her own cause? – and it was not long before she, Camille, openly declared her love to the sensitive and volatile composer. He immediately reciprocated, and in the weeks that followed the pair became lovers, and began to make preparations to marry (in that order). Berlioz's family was delighted with the news, but Camille's mother, clearly anxious to make a good marriage for her daughter and dubious about Berlioz's suitability as a son-in-law, expressed reluctance. Only if Berlioz could demonstrate the promise of professional success by procuring the Prix de Rome would she consent to the marriage.

Here, then, is the melodramatic supplement to the story of the 1830 prize competition – as though the outbreak of the July Revolution in the midst of it all were not dramatic enough. The sequel to the story of Berlioz's adventure with Camille is equally sensational, for the relationship was doomed to fail. As soon as Berlioz left for Italy, Camille's mother, worried about the modest income her prospective son-in-law could hope to receive from his father in La Côte-Saint-André, continued to search for a more assured match for her daughter, and found one in the wealthy piano manufacturer Camille Pleyel, who then married the extremely attractive young woman (who shared his first name) in 1831. But in the period between the Prix de Rome competition of 1830 and our composer's departure for Italy at the end of that year, Berlioz and Camille were lovingly devoted to one another, and excited and hopeful about their future.

The just-crowned laureate of the Institut de France immediately attempted to take advantage of his new-found stature to seek broader opportunities for performance in Paris. On 7 November 1830, at a benefit for the Opéra's pension fund, he arranged to have his newly completed *Ouverture de la Tempête* given at that theater (between the first act of Rossini's *Le Siège de Corinthe* and Hérold's ballet *La Somnambule*). This Overture, usually thought of as the work of the summer of 1830, was in fact conceived earlier for execution at the pianist-composer Ferdinand Hiller's concert at the Conservatoire on 10 January 1830[12] – and there is little doubt that its imaginative use of two pianos as purely orchestral instruments (a first of its kind) was inspired by, and intended for, Hiller, to whom he had confided the saga of his infatuation with Miss Smithson, and Hiller's *amie*, Camille Moke. In a program note prepared for the press, he detailed the unusual four-part structure of the Overture (*Introduction, Tempête, Action, Dénouement*) and gave a translation of the words sung by the small chorus: these were in Berlioz's own Italian (a language he was studying at the time) for the simple reason that the work was earlier scheduled for performance at the Théâtre Italien, where his friend Narcisse Girard conducted the orchestra, and where Italian was *de rigueur*. Here is a piece – his first important musical encounter with Shakespeare – that Berlioz surely hoped would have a separate existence as a concert overture. By using it as the finale of *Lélio ou le Retour à la vie*, however, he obscured the overture's original identity and inadvertently removed from circulation a fine work, which Camille Saint-Saëns rightly took to be the vocal and instrumental harbinger of the symphony that would come along at the end of the decade, *Roméo et Juliette*.

From October through December, Berlioz also attempted via letter and "pull" to obtain exemption from the Prix de Rome's obligation to go to Italy. He said that he would appeal to the King himself if he had to, and my assumption is that he did, for the archives are crowded with requests for exceptions of this sort.[13] But while the requirement to go to Germany was loosely enforced, no one seems to have escaped compulsory "exile" to Italy. French kings had been sending artists to Italy since the thirteenth century, and the rules for musicians were strictly modeled on those designed for practitioners of the visual arts. Roman musical life bore little resemblance to the majesty of the city's heritage in the realms of architecture, painting, and sculpture, of course, and in the nineteenth century it made little sense to send musicians there. The equivalent prize offered to musicians at the Conservatorio di Milano, for example, sent them to Germany and to France. Still, Berlioz's insistence on the absurdity of sending musicians to Rome had no effect on the authorities. As the Minister of the Interior, the Comte de Montalivet, wrote to the famous battle painter Horace Vernet, the then director of the French Academy in Rome, "it is upon the rigorous observation of the regulations that the future progress of art depends."[14] Thus, with a promise of fidelity from Camille that turned out to be less valuable than the six hundred francs from the Ministry which he received for the expedition, Berlioz made his "forced" departure from Paris on 31 December 1830.

The Symphonie fantastique

As the final step in his preparations for the Prix de Rome, Berlioz had hoped to give a concert on Ascension Day, 20 May 1830, at the Théâtre des Nouveautés, where his friend Nathan Bloc was the conductor of a thirty-three-man orchestra that would have had to be doubled for the grand occasion envisaged by the composer of the Symphonie fantastique. However, when the Théâtre Allemand was asked to give a command performance of Der Freischütz on that day, Berlioz was constrained to put off the concert until Pentecost, ten days later. He wrote to the hospital administration, as usual, requesting a reduction of the poor tax, and he wrote to the Prefect of Police, requesting the hall; the Prefect wrote to the director of the Opéra, Lubbert, and found that there was no objection.[15] But despite such laborious arrangements, musical and other, not everything could be put in place. Berlioz went to the country to visit the wealthy parents of one of his composition students, a Spaniard, and postponed the première until the fall.

After La Tempête was given at the Opéra, on 7 November 1830, Berlioz yet again set about preparing an "immense concert" to be given at the Conservatoire one month later, on 5 December. This would feature the *Francs-Juges* Overture, excerpts from the *Neuf Mélodies*, the prize cantata *Sardanapale* with the *Incendie* that had fizzled at the Institute, and, as *pièce de résistance*, the *Symphonie fantastique*. On the day of that concert, the magazine *Le Voleur* published a translation of the opening piece from E. T. A. Hoffmann's *Kreisleriana* ("Of Kapellmeister Johannes Kreisler's Musical Sorrows") and the *Mercure des salons*, in its current issue, published excerpts from a book on sorcery that included descriptions of opium taking, witches' dances, magic incantations, and other niceties of the day on which Satan assembled the faithful. Such literary fantasies and personifications of the romantic soul are deeply connected to Berlioz's first symphony. But we must remember that what was on everyone's mind during the opening months of the reign of Louis-Philippe, and particularly in the month of December, was in fact the fate of the ministers of the deposed King, Charles X. On 6 December, *Le Courrier français* went so far as to suggest that, given the overwhelming preoccupations of the public, new works would have little chance of any artistic or box-office success. With many revolutionaries demanding their heads, Polignac, Payronnet, Chantelauze, and Guernon-Ranville went on trial for their lives on the 15th (the day on which Lamartine published his "Ode contre la peine de mort"). On the 21st they learned that they would be not hanged, but incarcerated for life.

Berlioz had not been discouraged by warnings such as that of *Le Courrier français*, and in a gesture indicative of those freshly democratic times he invited the new King to the performance: "Hoping zealously to associate myself with the public expression of gratitude to the heroes of the national cause," his letter begins, "I am preparing a concert for the benefit of those wounded in July." After identifying himself as a recent winner of the Prix de Rome, Berlioz went on:

> Sire, the fine arts, too, have a role to play in enhancing the grandeur of our country. The enlightened manner in which Your Majesty has always honored them renders me confident that my request will not be considered improper, even were it not motivated by such a noble cause.

Although the King did not attend the concert, he did send Berlioz a generous honorarium of three hundred francs.[16]

The *Symphonie fantastique* represents a summing up of Berlioz's emotional and compositional initiation into the artistic world of Restoration Paris. Despite some shilly-shallying over the importance of the literary program with which the symphony was born, Berlioz clearly wished the work to tell a tale – of romantic desire, unrequited love, attempted suicide, imaginary murder, and hellish revenge – a tale that is continued in the sequel he assembled in 1831, *Le Retour à la vie*, which provides a logical continuation of the psychological progression in the life of the artist-hero of the *Fantastique*. The title generally associated with the *Symphonie fantastique* – "An episode in the life of an artist" – was, for Berlioz, at least from 1831 through 1835, in fact to apply to both works.

The "episode" is plainly linked to Berlioz's impossible passion for Harriet Smithson, by whom the youthful composer was smitten on 11 September 1827, when he saw her on the stage of the Odéon Theater in the role of Ophelia, opposite the Hamlet of Charles Kemble, in a production by a miscellaneous English company managed by William Abbot, with actors from several of the theaters of the English capital. After *Hamlet* on the 11th, Berlioz saw *Romeo and Juliet* on the 15th, with Smithson in the title role, and *Othello*, on the 18th, with Smithson as Desdemona. All the "young romantics" were in the audience for the English performances of Shakespeare – Hugo, Dumas, Delacroix, Vigny, Nerval – and all reveled in the very dramatic contrasts that had led the old-fashioned critics, following Voltaire, to think of Shakespeare as a barbarian.

In fact what they witnessed, despite the powerfully expressive acting of the members of the Kemble Company, was Shakespeare abridged and expurgated. In *Hamlet*, as we learn from the censor's report, the role of the priest was cut out, and "useless gossip," along with the "philosophical tirades that might have rendered the performance either boring or dangerous," was removed.[17] Nonetheless, the immensity of the drama and the intense beauty of the leading lady caused in Berlioz a whirlpool of emotion that fused Shakespearean poetry, dramatic music, and romantic love into – as he put it in the *Mémoires* – "the supreme drama" of his life.

In 1827 Berlioz was not inexperienced: after landing in Paris and setting up bachelor quarters with his cousin Alphonse Robert, he surely risked certain big-city pleasures that were unavailable in the puritanical province whence he came. He says nothing of this in correspondence, but the fact that his best friend's father thought of him as an adventurer suggests that copying scores at the Conservatoire was not his sole occupation in the mid-eighteen-twenties. Once, on 14 December 1825, Berlioz mentioned "une passion frénétique" to his home-town friend Édouard Rocher, which he overcame only by drowning himself in his music. If he had other affairs of the heart before the *coup de foudre* for Smithson, and it would be reasonable to assume that he did, we know nothing of them.

Whatever his previous escapades had been, Berlioz was simply and devastatingly bewitched by the lovely Irish actress. Forever more, he carried in his mind a kind of double *idée fixe* consisting of Shakespeare, who had illuminated for him the mystery of existence, and Smithson, who had brought the light to life. They were eventually to marry, then separate, and not without high emotion. But even in the rueful, waning days of their union, when he looked at his ill-starred wife, Berlioz was sometimes able to see in her a youthful Shakespearean heroine.

For two long years, Berlioz tells us, he suffered unrequited love, frequently unable to concentrate because of his longing for this far away woman who, like Estelle, was nearly four years his senior. He knew her only through her appearance, her movements on stage, and – importantly – the sound of her voice. He tried repeatedly, by letter and hand-delivered message, to approach "Miss Smithson," as she was always called in the press, only to be told that seeing the lady was simply out of the question.

By 1830, however, the woman whose mime and inflection had so fascinated a bevy of poets in 1827 was no longer able to command everyone's attention (the fashion for Shakespeare in English had subsided), and she was compelled to accept near-mute roles in now forgotten amusements at the Opéra Comique, where she would recite such lines as "Yes my William, cher enfant, mon fils chéri," as the English wife of a Frenchman. None the less, if Smithson's contract with the Opéra Comique turned out to be short-lived, it was not an ungenerous one: for taking part in productions of L'Auberge d'Auray, Jenny, and Les Deux Mots, she received thirty-five hundred francs per month[18] – fourteen times more than Berlioz's monthly stipend as winner of the Prix de Rome in the summer of that year, and a sign of the continuing respect in which she was held.

Smithson also took a role more worthy of her pantomimic talents, that of Fenella, in Auber's opera La Muette de Portici. In what is a quite remarkable coincidence, she appeared in this work at a concert at the Opéra for her own benefit on 5 December 1830 – the very day of the première at the Conservatoire of the Symphonie fantastique. As we have noted, Berlioz invited the King to his performance and received a royal honorarium of three hundred francs for his efforts; Harriet invited the King to her performance, too, and her royal honorarium – evidence of the relative standing of these two artists at the time, and of the two different theaters at which they appeared – came to a thousand francs.[19] The critic of the Journal des comédiens was unhappy that the administration of the Opéra had permitted a foreigner to enjoy the profits of such a benefit, especially one who could so easily have a number of brilliant engagements in her own country, but he was mistaken, for Smithson's career, unlike Berlioz's, was now on the wane.

There is "an entire Beethoven inside of this Frenchman" wrote the young German critic, Ludwig Börne, who was in Paris at the time of the première of the Symphonie fantastique. The others who issued critiques – I have found only five, a fraction of the forty or more that would have been common had this been the première of a new opera – were hesitantly appreciative of Berlioz's novel forms and uncommon sonorities. None shows any awareness that this first symphony would become the exordium of its composer's reputation and the emblem of nineteenth-century French instrumental music.

The *Symphonie fantastique* is a five-movement symphony loosely modeled on those of the classic masters, with an intellectual center of gravity at the outset (*Reveries, Passions*), and an exuberant farewell at the close (*Dream of a Witches' Sabbath*). Betwixt and between, a graceful dance (*A Ball*) and a pastoral episode (*Scene in the Country*) – both in ABA forms with introductions, transitions, and codas; and a stormy, multipartite procession (*March to the Scaffold*), also with introduction and coda, that ends on a dominant harmony and thus ushers in the finale. The similarities to Beethoven are undeniable, but the means by which Berlioz achieves continuity are radically different from those used by the man whose work has long *defined* our very notion of "symphony." Beethoven invented "pregnant" themes that give birth to a myriad of constituent elements which are combined, repeated, and brought to culmination in such a way that the process – "development" in a general sense – generates a tension-packed drama played out upon broadly contrasting tonal planes that undergird the structures of the movements both individually and as a group. Berlioz invented themes that are, by contrast, irregular, extended, and open-ended. The tonal plan of the *Fantastique*, with movements in C, A, F, G, and C, suggests allegiance to the classic norms (of dominant and subdominant relations), but also affection for the more "coloristic" relations (by third) that are often associated with the music of Schubert and the post-Beethoven generation.

Berlioz's most famous melody is the *idée fixe* – taken over from *Herminie*, the Prix de Rome cantata of 1828 – that runs through the five movements of this symphony. It is played in full as the principal theme of the first movement, and it is echoed in the four movements that follow, thus giving the work a cyclic unity of a purely architectural sort. Irregular in contour and phrase length, anguished and striving in emotional value, the tune in its original guise can hardly be called "lyrical," although it is texted, in *Herminie*, with words appropriate to its function in both works: "In vain I give voice to my evanescent plaint, I entreat him, he hears me not." Most observers have been struck by the asymmetry of the *idée fixe*, with its antecedent phrase of a conventional eight bars followed by a consequent phrase of not eight bars, as expected (particularly because it begins, like the antecedent, with an upbeat), but seven. When Robert Schumann wrote about Berlioz's first symphony in 1835, in an analysis that has never been surpassed, he discovered that normalcy here and elsewhere lay just beneath the surface: at first dumbfounded, Schumann soon perceived many of the ordered patterns that governed the work's larger proportions.

Symmetries, from the microscopic level to the grand scale, have always been the indispensable requirements of aesthetic worth. That they are not self-evident in Berlioz's œuvre has provided a special challenge to those who would characterize his style, which is pervaded by surprise in melody, harmony, rhythm, and sound. Harmonic sleights-of-hand and melodic deviations from the subcutaneous plane of expectations are techniques that Berlioz shared with all the composers of the classic-romantic continuum, of course, but listeners have too often been told, and too often believed, that there is something odd about his particular harmonic shifts and phraseological swerves – that they manifest plenty of genius, but not enough talent (whatever that puzzling if oft-repeated formulation may mean). At the end of the *Marche au supplice*, for example, there is a shocking move from the local tonality to the distant key of D flat. Now, there is also a shocking move to D flat at the coda of the *Eroica* Symphony's first movement. The circumstances are different, but the surprise is similar. Why is Beethoven not accused of having genius but lacking talent? Because of the historical forces (to which I shall return) that rendered his monumental catalogue of classical practice "normal," and thus, for most of his posthumous critics, beyond criticism. Nothing of Berlioz's practice became "normal" in this sense for the simple but profound reason that Berlioz tended not to repeat himself. There are many marches in Berlioz, but each, the *Marche au supplice* included, is a product of a unique idea, a solution to a problem posed only once.

What is perhaps most uncanny about Robert Schumann's analysis of the *Fantastique* – made after playing through Franz Liszt's extraordinary piano transcription (a testament to friendship if ever there was one) – is its perceptiveness regarding instrumentation, an aspect of his work that even Berlioz's enemies admired. Contrasting *pizzicato* and *arco* and *tremolo* strings in close proximity, doublings that cause two or more traditional instruments to sound ingeniously like one that is new, voices typically relegated to secondary roles (the English horn, the E flat clarinet, the percussion) brought to the fore as protagonists – these and other gestures were from the beginning the chemicals of Berlioz's creative laboratory and the compounds of his musical imagination. Not being a pianist, Berlioz was never tempted to conceive of musical textures as two handfuls of sound, or as prestidigitation sustained by a pedal. He was constrained, or rather liberated, to conceive of music as a tableau of instrumental colors in motion.

One of the most extraordinary colors of the *Fantastique* occurs in the finale, at the introduction of Berlioz's "burlesque parody" of the *Dies irae*. A funeral knell is sounded at this point by two large bells, pitched in C and G and tolling what may have been the pattern of some country church practice known to Berlioz in his youth. More than one modern orchestra has had bells specially cast for this singular moment, but in the score Berlioz suggests that, if bells are not available, several pianos may be used for the purpose. Indeed, though he heard the bells in his imagination and we hear them now in the concert hall and on disc, I believe that Berlioz himself never heard them in performance. They are nowhere mentioned in contemporary reviews, and this, had they sounded, would be odd indeed. (In later years, when Berlioz informed others of the instrumental forces required for the *Fantastique*, he mentioned not bells, but pianos.)

Those bells were to be placed *behind the scenes*, like the oboe at the opening of the third movement, and like so many other instruments and voices in Berlioz's œuvre that show the composer's spatial imagination at work. The hymn that they introduce, the Gregorian *Dies irae*, played by four bassoons and two ophicleides, becomes a principal theme of the movement. As the hallowed melody is repeated in shorter and shorter note-values, it progresses from the grave to the frivolous, leading some early reviewers aptly to use the words "impious," "heretical," and "licentious" in describing its use. In fact Berlioz takes segments from various parts of the liturgical tune, and not only its opening two phrases. It is highly unlikely that he opened the Gradual to refresh his recollection of the chant, because his habit, whether in music or poetry, was always to quote from memory. For some purists, however, perhaps the departure from the authority of tradition was yet another Berliozian sin.

It would be an historical misrepresentation to speak of the score of the Fantastique without discussing the literary narrative that Berlioz linked to this purely instrumental composition. And yet I am certain that it is possible to appreciate the work while knowing nothing of Chateaubriand, Hugo, Goethe, Harriet Smithson, and the Catholic Church. The delights of the music – the sudden textural and dynamic contrasts of the first and last movements, the crystalline orchestration of the second, with its brilliant counterpoint for the cornet (a part added as a second thought, but an inspiration of the first order), the sheer thrill of the brass in the march – are there for any open-minded listener to hear. It is no less the case, even if we are not bound by his "instructions," that Berlioz lavished considerable attention upon the program to which he connected the score. This compelling tale has a young composer afflicted with the emotional whirlpool that Chateaubriand called a vague des passions and captivated by a woman who refuses to return his love. Haunted by her image, which is inevitably accompanied in his mind by a curious melody, he attempts suicide by poisoning himself with opium (as did many a spurned lover of the time). Because the dose succeeds only in throwing him into a state of delirium, he imagines that he has killed his beloved, that he has been executed for committing the dastardly deed, and that he has yet again encountered the femme fatale, now a mere prostitute, as a participant in the devilish orgy of his funeral.

More than anything else, Berlioz's notoriety rests on this story, which is widely taken to represent his "infernal passion" for Harriet Smithson. He modified its details at least fourteen times – for fresh performance, for publication, and sometimes in order to bring it into line with the sequel, composed in the year following the symphony's première, and also later revised. The questions the story provokes today are the same as those it provoked in his own day, and fall, I think, into two realms. First, aesthetics – *can* instrumental music tell a story? And second, ethics – *should* it attempt to do so? To the second question, many might now say "Why not?" But verbs with moral overtones (*falloir, devoir*) were common in the musical parlance of the day and have been bandied about for centuries by opponents of modern music. When Berlioz urged Beethoven's Fifth Symphony upon his teacher, Lesueur, the latter listened in awe, but later said that such music *ought not* to be written. Similarly, on hearing Berlioz's first symphony in December 1830, a writer for the *Revue de Paris* said that one *ought not* to encourage such extra-musical baggage. We may know that overdoses of Beethoven and Berlioz produce no harmful side effects, but these critics were not so sure. Wagner's critics, too, were always full of shoulds and should-nots. (Thomas Mann parodied them in *The Buddenbrooks*, with his unforgettable portrait of the organist Edmund Pfühl, who was appalled by the madness and blasphemously perfumed "fog" of *Tristan*.) It is easy to dismiss such illiberal figures out of hand, but it is also too facile to say that moralistic criticism is always misguided.

As to the aesthetic problem of whether instrumental music *can* tell a story, the views are as numerous as the spectrum is colorful. Let it be said again that Berlioz's story echoes many sounds from the literature of his time. Among well-known writings, we may note Chateaubriand's *René* with its *vague des passions;* Hugo's *Ronde du sabbat* and *Dernier jour d'un condamné* with their particular morbidities; De Quincey's *Confessions of an Opium Eater* with its drug-induced dreams; and Balzac's "l'Opium" (published in *La Caricature* on 11 November 1830, less than a month before the symphony's première) with its evocation of the excitement and voluptuousness of taking the drug. We may also note Goethe's *Sorrows of Young Werther* (whose hero's dejected gloom is rekindled on hearing "that old tune" played on regular occasion by his beloved Charlotte) and, of course, *Faust* (where Gretchen, in the delirious vision of the final scene, alludes to the tolling of the bells as she sees herself carried to her own public execution). Among the lesser lights that may also have found reflection here, one commands particular attention. Louis Lanfranchi's *Voyage à Paris* (1830) features an "Episode de la vie d'un voyageur" in which a young man wanders round Paris in search of a beautiful woman whose image comes before his mind's eye, "like an *idée fixe*," whenever he sees a rose. (Years later, in the last chapter of the *Mémoires*, Berlioz, too, declares that a rose always produced in him the vague feeling of poetic love.)

The *rêveries* and *passions* of the first movement of the *Fantastique* – its solitary dreams and intimations of ardor – are therefore the very stuff of the romantic era; this almost goes without saying. The *bal* of the second was a hallmark of the social life of the capital – Berlioz went to balls during his early years in Paris and reported to his family on their delights and distresses, there were several spectacular masquerades at the Opéra at the beginning of 1830, and high-society dancing-parties were common. Ball scenes are crucial symbols of the social order in such novels of the period as Stendhal's *Le Rouge et le noir* (1831) and Balzac's *Le Père Goriot* (1834), to say nothing of an even more famous novel with an even more famous *scène de bal*, Flaubert's *Madame Bovary* (1857). That Berlioz should "take" the image of Harriet to the ball in his program – or to the country, as he does in the third movement's *Scène aux champs* – requires little imagination. (Taking Faust to the plains of Hungary, as he does at the opening of *La Damnation de Faust*, requires more.)

The opium eating that precedes the *Marche au supplice* was then a widespread medicinal practice: Berlioz's father was expert at it, took the drug in quantity to quell his own suffering, and left an unfinished treatise on the subject at his death.[20] The word *supplice* can mean tor-

4   *La Valse*, a lithograph by J.-E.-V. Arago adorning an album of *romances* by A.-P.-J. Doche (1799–1849). *Un Bal* in the *Symphonie fantastique* evokes the same image.

ture of a public sort, and punishment as public spectacle had for some time been much in vogue. Lastly, prostitution, evoked in the finale (where the pristine Madonna has become the proverbial whore), was always on view in Paris, and was nowhere more in evidence than in the galleries of the Palais Royal, at the foot of the rue de Richelieu, where the music publisher Maurice Schlesinger had his printing shop (the city's best known gathering place and gossip mill for musicians) and where Berlioz lived for the three years prior to his departure for Rome.

Some of Berlioz's explicitly musical biography is embodied within the symphony, of course, in the form of a series of self-borrowings, such as the opening melody of the introduction to the first movement, which was taken from a song composed in his youth; the *Scène aux champs*, taken from the *Gratias* of the early *Messe solennelle*; the *idée fixe*, from *Herminie*; and the *Marche au supplice*, from *Les Francs-Juges* – to say nothing of the more generally liberating energies he felt after hearing "that awe-inspiring giant" who was Beethoven. But it is his emotional biography that has been most talked about as central to the work – his unrequited love for Harriet Smithson, that is, which he was able to exorcise from his mind only with assistance from Camille Moke, whose tattle shattered Berlioz's image of the actress as immaculate and pure. (On their wedding night the image was conclusively restored.) Freed from Harriet's grip, at least temporarily, in the spring of 1830, he was able to set down the program and the music with a cool head and a sure hand.

There is no doubt, then, that Berlioz drew on personal experience in constructing the narrative of the *Symphonie fantastique*. But, as Balzac reminds us in *La Peau de Chagrin*, written at the same time as the symphony, "it is very difficult to persuade the public that an author can conceive of a crime without himself being a criminal."[21] Still, persuade the public one must. For it is wrong to read Berlioz's "real life" through the program of this symphony as though it were some sort of transparent, court-room confession. The document – conditioned both by life and by the literature that shaped experience into composition – had, in the end, to satisfy the demands of art.

2 Innovation (1830–1848)

Revolution in France, reaction in Italy

The three-day revolution that sacked Charles X and that opened the way to the "bourgeois" monarchy of Louis-Philippe was caused by Charles's overly zealous attempts to limit the rights guaranteed by the Constitutional Charter of 1814, to control the legislature, to protect the Church, and to muzzle the press. When the hostilities broke out, on 27 July 1830, the King was in the country – and Berlioz was in a tiny cell under the dome of the Palais de l'Institut, finishing his prize cantata, *Sardanapale*. The composer later told his father that he left the Institute on the 29th, found a rifle, and prepared to join those who were battling in the streets – workers, students, republicans, Bonapartists, members of the National Guard, and others shooting at the Louvre from the very left-bank terrace upon which he emerged – in order, as he put it, to help "regain our freedom." Apparently delighted with the flight of Charles X and, soon thereafter, with the inauguration of the new King, Louis-Philippe I, he declared to his sister, on 5 September, that the revolution was "made for the liberation of the arts," adding, "I will succeed ten times sooner than I would have" had this revolution not occurred. Berlioz did indeed enjoy a great deal of success in the eighteen-thirties and beyond. But the success he spoke of here – conventional, commanding, pecuniary success – was measured at the Académie Royale de Musique (the Opéra), and there, as we shall see, he was to have no luck.

Berlioz was chagrined not to have participated more actively in the fighting. From his letters one can sense the acute desire he felt actually to pull the trigger and draw blood. In fact Charles's army was weak, uncommitted, and much diminished by defection; the blood-shedding, though severe, was brief. Still, if Berlioz's encounter with this decisive moment in French history was disappointing to him, it would none the less be envied by some of his contemporaries: Edgar Quinet and Prosper Mérimée, for example, both later regretted not having been present at this "extraordinary performance," at one of those rare moments in history when the old seems to give way to the new. Richard Wagner, then an impressionable boy of seventeen, said that the uprising caused the world of history to come alive: "Naturally I became a fervent partisan of the revolution," he wrote, "which I now regarded as an heroic, popular and victorious struggle, unstained by the terrible excesses of the first French revolution."[1] "No excesses!" exclaimed Heinrich Heine, likewise thrilled by the insurrection; "A new France begins [. . .] There is a continuous playing of violins up above in heavenly blue jubilation."[2]

Such favorable sentiments towards the new monarchy were widely shared in the French artistic community, even if the classes represented in the legislature – land owners and professional men – remained much the same as they had been under Charles X. Honoré de Balzac was therefore less optimistic than Berlioz about the revolution, writing in his *Lettres sur Paris* the very words that Berlioz would later write at the opening of his *Mémoires*: "As for the theaters, literature, poetry, all of that is now dead." But Berlioz did not think so, greeting the new régime in the autumn of 1830 with an arrangement for double chorus and orchestra of Rouget de Lisle's patriotic hymn, *La Marseillaise* (which he dedicated to that poet-musician), and with an arrangement of Rouget's *Chant du neuf Thermidor*, which one might wish to see as a musical recognition of the end of a "reign of terror," like the original, and as appropriate to the day on which Louis-Philippe officially became King of the French: not 9 *Thermidor* (27 July 1794), but 9 *August* 1830.

La Marseillaise was for some months the favorite of all those who could compose, as though it were the propeller of the soul of the nation, long suppressed, now set free. Berlioz's contemporary, Adolphe Adam, wrote a piano fantasy on Rouget de Lisle's famous tune, and made his own orchestral arrangement as well (although it is Berlioz's version that is now the official French national anthem). *Chansons* glorifying recent events also poured forth in quantity. Such immediate musical manifestations, whether motivated by political conviction or expedience, were equally matched in the world of the visual arts: at the artistic Salon, in 1831, at least twenty-two paintings were put on display that illustrated the three-day revolution, among them Delacroix's great allegory of Liberty leading the people. (Delacroix had also participated in the fighting, even while working on the *Bataille de Nancy* that had been commissioned by the deposed Charles X.)

Berlioz's optimism at the advent of the reign of Louis-Philippe was overshadowed by the reluctance he felt on leaving Paris, and Camille, at the end of 1830. He lingered in the capital until New Year's Eve, then made his way home to La Côte-Saint-André, where he delayed his departure for Rome until the second week of February. He was burdened outwardly with rounds of family visits, and inwardly with various thoughts of gloom and doom. In letters to friends he spoke of his painful separation from his fiancée; to Ferdinand Hiller, on 23 January 1831, he explicitly mentioned Camille's knowledge of his total devotion to her, and he added, quite mysteriously, that there was one tremendous sacrifice, "the greatest of all," that he would be willing to perform, should the need arise. We simply have no notion of what this great sacrifice might have been. Robbery? Murder? Suicide? Even more enigmatic is what he wrote to Hiller one week later, when he said that he was obliged to conceal from everyone *except* Camille some sort of terrible anguish – a *chagrin affreux* – of which, again, we have no knowledge at all.

The intense intimacy of Berlioz's feelings for his beloved was shattered in mid-April, after he had been in Italy, at the French Academy in

Rome, for six or seven weeks. Anxiety-ridden at having heard nothing from Camille since his departure from France, Berlioz was already homeward bound when he received a letter from Mme Moke coolly informing him that her daughter was to marry the wealthy piano-maker, Camille Pleyel. For several days, he literally suffered from convulsions, as moments of lucidity followed upon moments of rage; at one point, in despair, he threw himself into the sea. He was the victim not only of an abuse of confidence but of a "hideous crime," he recounted in letters to his family and friends; he had been charmed by a "rattle snake" who was nothing but a little girl "with neither heart nor soul." He planned to take revenge by returning to Paris, to gain entrance to the Mokes' apartment by disguising himself as a lady's maid, and there, before committing suicide, "to kill without compunction two guilty women" – Camille and her treacherous mother – "and one innocent man" – if not Camille's father, presumably Pleyel himself.

Unlike the contemporary letters, the account of this drama, in the *Mémoires*, written over ten years after the event, is comically melodramatic, carefully blending the author's madness with concern for his music – the score of the *Fantastique*, that is, which he had been revising in the first months of 1831:

> I put the score of the symphony in an envelope, addressed it to Habeneck, and threw it into a valise with a few clothes. I had with me a pair of double-barreled pistols, which I loaded; and I examined and put into my pocket two small bottles of refreshment – laudanum and strychnine. Reassured as to my arsenal, I went out again to await my departure, wandering aimlessly through the streets of Florence with the sickly, restless, and frightening air of a mad dog.

When he came to his senses, Berlioz made his way to Nice, where Shakespeare came to the rescue: he read *King Lear* and set down the *Grande Ouverture du Roi Lear*, whose autograph is dated 7 May 1831, and whose stern and vigorous character reflects the quality of the play. He also sketched an *Intrata di Rob-Roy MacGregor*, whose title derives from

Sir Walter Scott. (Played by the Société des Concerts in April 1833, the work, "long and diffuse" by the composer's own admission, was then retired from use.) In Nice he also put an end to the celibacy he had maintained since June 1830 (when he had last enjoyed the favors of Camille) with an Italian woman of unknown identity. The encounter was *al fresco* because the professional credentials of his inamorata were such that he thought better of taking her to his rooms:

> I took her into a cave I knew at the edge of the ocean. But upon entering, I heard a growl from deep inside, which I thought was some sailor who was sleeping there, or perhaps it was Caliban himself. We yielded the terrain to him and celebrated our nuptials farther down on the open shore. The sea was furious, the waves were breaking at our feet, the nocturnal wind was wild, and I cried out with Chactas, "O Splendid nuptial rites, worthy of the grandeur of our untamed loves."[3]

"So you see that I am cured," he told his friends in Paris, and by June, back at the French Academy in Rome, he was sufficiently composed to transform his recent experiences into an original work of art. This was a *mélologue* (an admixture of monologue and music), *Le Retour à la vie*, later baptized *Lélio*, which became the "conclusion and complement" to the *Symphonie fantastique*. Transforming the symphony's nightmarish vision into a rational expression of faith in the power of music, with spoken monologues introducing and linking six varied musical numbers, the sequel became the controversial vehicle with which Berlioz jump-started his career on returning to Paris in the autumn of 1832.

It is tempting to suggest that this new composition, with its sermons on love and adventure, was purely autobiographical. But this is to ignore the complexity of the borrowings it contains from Berlioz's own music (the second number, a *Chorus of Shades*, is the *Méditation* from the 1829 prize cantata; the finale is the Overture to the *Tempest* from the summer of 1830), and of the echoes it carries from his own letters as well as from the writings of Thomas Moore (from whom he adopted the genre of the melologue), Shakespeare, and Victor Hugo. As in the *Symphonie fantastique*, here, too, personal experience was combined with artistic instruction and rigor in such a way as to produce a work that is peculiar, to be sure, but that is consistent, and effective when performed with vim.

Only a few weeks after putting the finishing touches on the *mélologue*, Berlioz manifested a renewed interest in the larger social issues of the day in a curious letter that he wrote from Rome, in July 1831, to Charles Duveyrier, one of the Saint-Simonian reformers, who had lately purchased the Parisian newspaper *Le Globe* to preach their utopian doctrines. The letter is curious because it is practically the sole evidence we have of Berlioz's express concern with the obliteration of privilege and the betterment of the poor. "As concerns the political reorganization of society," he wrote, "I am today convinced that Saint-Simon's program is the only one that is complete, and true." The day on which the letter was written, 28 July 1831 – the anniversary to the day of the 1830 Revolution – might have inflamed his spirits and exaggerated his desire to join his efforts to those of the Saint-Simonians, for when the movement transformed itself into a church, or cult, Berlioz became a swift and willing excommunicate.

Be this as it may, the Austrian Chancellor's secret police intercepted Berlioz's letter, and Metternich himself, on 18 August 1831, advised his ambassador in Rome to be wary of the "dangerous tendencies towards fanaticism" of this "young follower of the Saint-Simonian doctrine," to refuse permission should he wish to travel in Austrian territory (which included at the time much of northern Italy), and to inform the Vatican of the nefarious influence he might possibly exert on his fellow students. This gives credence to the amusing story Berlioz tells in chapter 44 of the *Mémoires* about the second number of *Le Retour à la vie*, the *Chœur d'ombres*, originally written in a fantastical and imaginary language that the composer called "an ancient dialect from the north" ("O sonder foul, sonder foul leimi," etc.). Fearing that the text contained a radical political message, the Papal authorities delayed authorization to publish until they were satisfied that it resembled no language intelligible to man. Only then, Berlioz writes, was "the Chorus of Shades printed." Now, no such Italian printing has ever been found, and I doubt that it ever existed. But it is perfectly possible that his "language of the dead" caused genuine suspicion at a time when the not yet settled régime in France was highly unsettling to her neighbors.

The rich texture of Berlioz's life in Italy in the first half of 1832 – visiting the cities of Rome, Naples, and Florence, wandering the backwoods with rifle and guitar, observing the customs and enjoying the sights – must have been the stuff of many of the conversations he had on returning to La Côte, in June, for an agreeable five-month stay with his family that was untroubled by the tensions of the period before the Prix de Rome. It was then, and there, in hiding (for the rules prescribed that he should spend two years in Italy, while he had spent only fifteen months), that Berlioz prepared another "return to life" – this one to the capital city, whose rhythms and patterns and habits of thought exerted such gravitational pull on the composer that he would remain *parisien*, despite the temptation of orbits abroad, for the next thirty-six years.

The composer in Paris

Berlioz's plan had been to give a *grand concert dramatique* in Paris before departing, again, for the year in Germany stipulated by the regulations of the Prix de Rome. His stature as a returning laureate helped him to secure the concert hall at the Conservatoire, hire an orchestra of a hundred enthusiastic players from the Opéra and Société des Concerts, and engage the almighty Habeneck to conduct. On 9 December 1832, the now complete *Épisode de la vie d'un artiste*, consisting of the *Symphonie fantastique* and *Le Retour à la vie*, was given for the first time to an audience of artists, writers, connoisseurs, aristocrats, journalists, and fans. Over twenty reviews appeared in the press, and these describe reactions to Berlioz's production that range from admiration to contempt. The latter emotion was expressed by F.-J. Fétis, whom

5 Berlioz in Rome in 1831. Émile Signol's small portrait is characteristic of those
   made by (and of) the winners of the Prix de Rome.

Berlioz had explicitly satirized in *Le Retour à la vie*, in a monologue
regarding artistic integrity, for having suggested "improvements" to
the symphonies of Beethoven. (Fétis's vituperative reaction eventually
had the salutary result of provoking a brilliant response from the pen

of Robert Schumann, as well as Eduard Hanslick's thoughtful commentary of some years later.)

Berlioz revised *Le Retour à la vie* for performance in Weimar, in 1855, after which time he added a name for its artist-hero, *Lélio*, to the title. But the work never made an impact greater than it did on the afternoon of 9 December 1832. In addition to the accolades he received on that occasion from Liszt, Paganini, Chopin, and the other celebrated figures in the hall, Berlioz also received the compliments of Harriet Smithson. (It was the publisher, Maurice Schlesinger, who had had the idea of inviting her to the concert.) When the actress, herself recently returned to Paris, heard the narrator of the *mélologue* reciting Berlioz's words of unrequited love –

> Oh, if I could but find this Juliet, this Ophelia, for whom my heart cries out! If I could but partake of that rapture tainted by sorrow that gives forth true love!

– she appears to have realized that the object of this love was none other than herself.

Accordingly, on 15 December 1832, some fifteen years after his teenage flirtation with Estelle Dubœuf, seven years after a short-lived Parisian *passion frénétique*, and eighteen months after he laid to rest the "violent distraction" of Camille Moke with a spree by the sea at Nice, Berlioz finally made the acquaintance, in person, of Harriet Constance Smithson. She had returned to Paris in the autumn of 1832 with the hope of rekindling the enthusiasm for English theater that had made her so successful in 1827. In the midst of her struggles with French officialdom for support of her new theatrical venture, she had gone with a friend to the Conservatoire to hear Berlioz's concert. The note of congratulations that she sent to him after the concert lit the long and sometimes fickle fuse of a firecracker that nearly fizzled but finally discharged, ten months later, in the variegated colors of matrimony. Berlioz responded to Harriet's note with a passionate response beseeching her to allow him to call. Two weeks later he was telling Liszt that he was yet again intoxicated with love, and that his love, this time, was truly returned. He postponed the trip to Germany and he began, again, to think of marriage.

By French law, men over twenty-five could marry against the wishes of their parents only after having officially requested their consent via an *acte respectueux* prepared by a notary. Not once, but three times, between February and June of 1833, Berlioz's father rejected his son's formal appeals to marry Miss Smithson. Meanwhile the prospective bride became doubtful, the groom, impatient, the situation tense. At the beginning of March, returning from an audience with the Minister of Commerce, Harriet caught her dress while stepping down from her carriage and suffered a terrible broken leg. The accident was painful, figuratively as well as literally, for it led to the cancellation of a performance planned for her benefit and to a break in the momentum, weak though it was, of the revival of her career.

Hector's devotion to the actress caused renewed estrangement from his family. Why did his parents, who had so warmly welcomed the engagement to Camille, so strongly reject the pledge to Harriet? In certain circles, after all, marriage to an English woman, like the English riding habit, was popular: Lamartine, Vigny, and Tocqueville all married English women, and perhaps they, like Berlioz, were also inspired by Shakespeare, whose female characters were then viewed as "angels of purity and paragons of fidelity."[4] But in the nineteenth-century French provinces (Berlioz's family demonstrates the point to perfection), the morals of real English women were seen as even more loose than those of the Parisians.[5] As a result, Berlioz's father and mother, his sister Nanci and his uncle Félix Marmion, all seem to have believed that Smithson (whose first name Berlioz always Frenchified as Henriette), an actress no less, must have been of particularly dubious morality. Worse, she came with no dowry – something Berlioz's father would naturally have hoped for from his son's wife in order to provide the same for his daughters.

This created a vicious circle, for the fact that Berlioz could not count on receiving an income from his father augmented Harriet's own doubts about the marriage, which were already exacerbated by the continued needling of her sister, her constant companion, whom Berlioz uncharitably called that "damned little hunchback." We may fairly wonder, then, how the lovers actually communicated, and thus how well they actually came to know one another, for the first attraction had been spiritual, not carnal, and there had not been one of those heated exchanges of letters by which the temperature of so many romances is raised. Berlioz knew little English at the time, and Harriet's French was far from fluent: she spoke the language, but "unfortunately," as Berlioz wrote six years later, she "was never able to learn French well enough to speak it on the stage."

At the end of August 1833, at the end of his tether because of Harriet's vacillations, Berlioz threatened to go off to Germany, this time with a wayward young chorus girl whom "fate," he told Ferrand, had thrown into his arms. Only then did Smithson finally decide to fix the date. On 2 October 1833 the couple, in the presence of the bride's sister, Anne Cecilia, and her friend Thomas Mills, signed a marriage contract at the office of the Parisian notary Augustin-Jules Guyot. The contract stipulated that debts contracted prior to the marriage were not to become the responsibility of the other party (although years later Berlioz told his son that he paid Harriet's debts of fourteen thousand francs and sent money to her mother as well), and it stipulated that all subsequently acquired wealth and property was to be shared. On the following day the marriage was "solemnized in the House of his Excellency the British Ambassador at the Court of France" by the Chaplain in residence there, the Reverend H. Luscombe. Smithson's witnesses were Bertha Stritch and Robert Cooper (English friends from the theater?); Berlioz's were Jacques Strunz (the little-known violinist, composer, and journalist) and his confidant in matters of the heart, Franz Liszt.[6] Six months after their brief honeymoon in Vincennes, the newlyweds – short of money and "overwhelmed by visitors" – moved into inexpensive lodgings in Montmartre, then still a village just north of the city limits; two years later they moved back in town.

By the time of her marriage to Berlioz, Harriet, at thirty-three, was no longer young by the standards of the day, and her sexual innocence, for a woman of the theater, was uncommon. Since it is likely that she had many suitors, we may well wonder whether she had difficulty giving herself to a man, something that could explain, better than those financial incertitudes, her reticence to marry Berlioz even after declaring her love. None the less her new husband did break her carnal fast, and a son was duly born to the couple, ten months later, on 14 August 1834, at 11 am, in their house at Montmartre. On the birth certificate,[7] the infant's father is listed as being thirty-one and a half years old (he was not yet thirty-one), his mother, as thirty-two and a half (she was two years older). Did the pair prefer to be seen as closer in age than they were? Nine days later, on 23 August 1835, at Saint-Pierre de Montmartre, the baby was baptized Louis-Clément-Thomas Berlioz, [8] though his parents called him only Louis, and all subsequent biographers have followed suit. Berlioz's old friend Thomas Gounet, who had lent him money at the time of the wedding, accepted the responsibilities of godfather.

For the next four or five years, Berlioz made efforts to integrate his wife into his increasingly active professional life: he spoke to Victor Hugo, Alfred de Vigny, George Sand, and Alexandre Dumas about possible dramatic roles for Harriet, and he assisted her to perform on several occasions through 1837. At mid-decade there was talk of a tour in England and of a tour in America, but no such travel ever materialized, for when one partner wished to go, the other wished to remain. Still, at that time, the prospects of the young *ménage* seemed bright.

As a composer, Berlioz became known early on for his energy, his emotional intensity, his opposition to the status quo. But this did not mean that he was an advocate of all that was wild and free. Quite to the contrary, Berlioz was a highly disciplined musician whose expressive materials resulted from extensive premeditation. Nor will the apparently contradictory charge, that he obeyed the tenets of some sort of bizarre "system," hold up in court. If that word applies, it is not in the pejorative sense intended by the critics, for his "system" was to avoid cliché like the plague, to eschew heart-on-sleeve confession, and to express emotion in ways that were unusual, yet never without order. In an era that prized damp eyes, Berlioz's, *in the workshop*, and *on the podium* (see illustration 8), were almost always clear and dry.

The first major work to come from his pen, after his marriage, provides a good example of the "systematic" behavior to which I allude. This was his second symphony, completed in Montmartre on 22 June 1834. Berlioz first mentioned it in January, in a letter to Joseph d'Ortigue: "You know that I am writing a piece for chorus, orchestra, and solo viola for Paganini. He himself came to ask me for it several days ago." The chorus disappeared, the projected number of movements expanded from one or two to four, and an association was made – but only *after* the work was fully drafted – with the melancholic persona that Lord Byron had constructed for himself in *Childe Harold's Pilgrimage* (1818). The second, third, and fourth movements did indeed carry programmatic titles from the beginning – *Marche de pèlerins chantant la prière du soir*, *Sérénade d'un montagnard des Abruzzes à sa maîtresse*, *Orgie de brigands* – but the first, *Harold aux montagnes*, and the work as a whole, were titled only in the final stages of composition. Berlioz did once say that Byron was among the poets who had influenced him most, but those who may think that this symphony exemplifies his role as a composer of "illustrative music" must think again, for what is illustrated is less Byron's poem than Berlioz's own Italian experiences (of pilgrims and madonnas) and imaginings (of pirates and debauchery) as colored by his familiarity with Byronic imagery and technique.

The four-movement design of *Harold en Italie* is conventionally Beethovenian, and the parade of reminiscences found in the finale is explicitly derived from Beethoven's Ninth Symphony (which Berlioz heard for the first time in January 1834). But the rhythms are novel, and the orchestration – with a part for solo viola that modestly comments on the action (too modestly for Paganini, who first thought the part unchallenging) – is unique. Ever since the première of the work, which took place on 23 November 1834, the second-movement *Pilgrims' March* has been of special interest. When the symphony was performed in its entirety, this movement occasionally had the honor of being repeated. Berlioz frequently performed it as a separate entity, as he did in Brussels in the autumn of 1842, for example, when he then presented a manuscript copy, with a dedication, to the Belgian King Léopold I. The movement was also transcribed for piano and separately published by Franz Liszt. (This is presumably what the organist played at Berlioz's funeral, when the *Marche* served as the postlude.) Writing to Humbert Ferrand, the eventual dedicatee of the full score, on 16 May 1834, Berlioz expressed the hope, which came true, that this movement in particular would achieve special renown.

The movement is in three large sections: March, "Trio," March. The march theme itself consists of a series of like, eight-bar phrases, each ending on a different, and sometimes distant, degree of the scale, each ushered home to the key of E major with the same remarkable harmonic sleight of hand – a low hoot on C, a high chime on B. The central section is a *Canto religioso*, or chorale, with arpeggios for the solo viola played *sul ponticello* while the rhythm of the march continues, *pizzicato*, in the bass. The march returns, highly abbreviated, and a Coda rounds off the movement, with a reminiscence of the arpeggios of the Trio now played not *sul ponticello* but in *posizione normale*, thus supplying a sonorous resolution to the earlier, sizzled accents of the solo instrument that provide the most curious sonority of the symphony as a whole. The entire movement is dynamically shaped as a *soufflet*, as a lengthy crescendo followed by a somewhat shorter diminuendo, as the pilgrims may be imagined to arrive from and recede into the distance. Wagner borrowed this idea for his own Pilgrims' March, in *Tannhäuser*, but what comes to the fore in the Berlioz is the clarity of the design of the principal melody, for it is as though he contrived the pattern first, then shaped the tune to fit.

Or, one might say, he devised a structure with the properties of poetry, then clothed it in music with the properties of prose. He assigned this movement to the category of the *nocturne*, and in 1863 associated it with other music we shall have occasion to mention here: the Adagio of *Roméo et Juliette*, the duet in Act IV of *Les Troyens*, and the duet in Act I of *Béatrice et Bénédict*. He might also have associated it with the *Prière* in Act II of *Benvenuto Cellini*, where a chorus of pilgrims literally passes beneath the windows of Cellini's studio: there, monks' prayers are joined to those of Cellini's beloved Teresa and his apprentice Ascanio in a series of regular phrases couched in the very key, not by coincidence, of the *Marche de pèlerins*. In the *Prière*, we arrive by malice aforethought at the distant degrees of D, G, C, and F – not one of which is found in the E major scale – and return home to E, as in *Harold*, in a way that calculation causes to appear effortless. The application of the word "systematic" to this kind of writing, far from pejorative, is apt, I think, and complimentary.

When Berlioz was engaged in his unsuccessful attempt to obtain an exception to the rules that obliged winners of the Prix de Rome to spend two years in Italy, in the autumn of 1830, he addressed an appeal directly to King Louis-Philippe, presumably the first time that he made contact with the head of the Orléans branch of the royal family. He later had a number of agreeable encounters with Louis-Philippe's sons, and in retrospect – from the darker days of the Second Empire – he looked back upon the House of Orléans with regret at its passing from the scene. Of the members of that family, it was the eldest son, Ferdinand-Philippe, the new Duc d'Orléans, who became the greatest friend of the arts (see illustration 6). Harriet Smithson had twice solicited the Duc's patronage for performances she gave in 1833, and Berlioz had solicited it for a concert and dramatic representation that he gave, with Harriet, on 24 November of that year. Now, about to the give the première of *Harold en Italie*, he again sought the privilege of the Duc's benefaction. Going well beyond the typical letter of solicitation to honor a concert by appearing in the house, the letter that Berlioz addressed to the Duc d'Orléans, on 17 November 1834, offers a kind of emotional summing-up at a time, two days after moving his family from Montmartre back to Paris, that suggests a graceful familiarity with the member of the royal family who was, let it not be forgotten, the heir to the throne of France.

> Monseigneur,
> Would it be ill-advised for an artist whose career is held back by innumerable difficulties that torment but do not dishearten him to seek the support of an august patron? Your Royal Highness has too often displayed all that a young person could hope for by way of

generous understanding for me not to be emboldened to approach him as I do now. It is hardly likely, Monseigneur, that my name has come to Your Highness's attention without the accompanying epithets of "lunatic" and "eccentric." Though I hear repeatedly from my friends and from that infinitesimally small segment of the public referred to as my "fanatics" that such reproaches of lunacy and eccentricity have from time immemorial been addressed to artists who stray ever so slightly from the beaten track, it is still no less the case that almost all the avenues to success are closed to me by an endless and indefatigable opposition.

I come therefore, Monseigneur, to beseech Your Royal Highness to have the goodness to attend the concert that I intend to give at the Conservatoire and for which I herewith enclose the program. Perhaps, after having heard my music performed by one-hundred-and thirty young persons all of whom are more or less touched by the same disequilibrium that is attributed to me, Your Highness will decide for himself, as my friends have done, that a room at Charenton is not what I most urgently need. Obstinate as I am, and determined to work towards my goal with ironclad perseverance, even if I should have to claw the way for myself with teeth and nails through gates which refuse to open, I firmly believe that one day I shall succeed. Unfortunately, that day may come only at a time when I no longer have teeth and nails, and this is a horrible thought for an artist who feels himself in the fullness of his creativity, and who fears that henceforth his creative powers can only decline.

I should be delighted, Monseigneur, if Your Highness were willing to grant me a moment of his time and come to judge *for himself* whether I am or am not worthy of his noble protection.

Here we find an expression of Berlioz's trust in the Prince's artistic understanding, as well as a demonstration of his own frankness, self-awareness, ready humor, and confidence. The prediction of future success that we see in this letter can be found elsewhere in Berlioz's writings. But the sharp contrast between frustration and ambition, the detached poet's superimposition of self-mockery upon heartfelt sincerity, the use of the word *fou* (crazy) to foreshadow mention of the crazy-house (Charenton) and the mention of teeth and nails as symbols of struggle and old age – these are the elements of Berlioz's finest literary style.

Educated at the Collège Henry IV, a public school, and in music, dance, and drawing by a series of private tutors including the painters Ary Scheffer and Newton Fielding, Ferdinand-Philippe was well equipped to appreciate the flowering of French romanticism in the eighteen-thirties. Evidence of this comes from Victor Hugo, who in his funeral oration for the Duc mentioned his love of arts and letters, and from Berlioz's friend Jules Janin, who considered the Prince an intellectual and a sincere friend of liberty. It emerges as well from the records of his commissions and the quality of the paintings in his private collection; from countless requests for patronage, preserved in the archives, in the hands of painters and sculptors and musicians alike; and in particular from the extraordinary series of letters, such as this one, that Berlioz himself addressed to His Royal Highness from the autumn of 1833 until the summer of 1842, when the Duc d'Orléans accepted the dedication of the *Symphonie funèbre et triomphale* shortly before he was killed in a freak accident, leaping from a runaway carriage, on 13 July 1842.

That Berlioz genuinely respected Ferdinand-Philippe's taste is clear: when the Duc subscribed to Berlioz's concert of 25 November 1838 with a generous *encouragement* of five hundred francs, Berlioz expressed profound gratitude for His Highness's renewed expression of interest:

> You have done me the honor of explaining, Monseigneur, that advanced musical study has been foreign to your experience. But this admission has in no way diminished my ardent desire to have you hear my compositions, convinced as I am of the capacity of certain elevated souls to distinguish the principal characteristics of every work of art worthy of the name.[9]

Berlioz's words constitute not flattery, but faith.

During the four decades of his public career, Berlioz gave several hundreds of concerts at home and abroad, and became a concert-giving

6 Ferdinand-Philippe, Louis-Philippe's eldest son, who assumed the title of
Duc d'Orléans in 1830, when his father became King of the French.
Alexandre Fiochi's portrait was made some ten years later.

"institution" in his own right. Viewed from afar, the nearly simultaneous opening of Berlioz's concert career and the foundation of the
Société des Concerts du Conservatoire, in 1828, would seem to have
been propitious for the formation of a natural alliance: here was a
French composer who could take up the symphony where Beethoven

had left it, and who could thereby provide the new symphonic organization with native French food for thought. But the Société, destined to become the greatest orchestra in Europe for decades to come, was from the beginning an inherently conservative organization whose guiding spirit, François-Antoine Habeneck, was a monotheist: "Credo in unum deum," he would have said. That god was Beethoven and Beethoven alone.

The Société des Concerts did undertake a smattering of works by younger composers, among them Georges Onslow, Louise Farrenc, and Felix Mendelssohn, but it shunned Berlioz after performing the *Rob Roy* Overture in 1833, presumably because of the hostile relations that developed between its headstrong conductor and the equally determined young composer. Berlioz did not like the "modifications" of classic works that Habeneck performed, and Habeneck did not like the modifications of classic norms that Berlioz incorporated in his music. As one of the Société's historians later explained, Berlioz was perceived as having "almost destroyed the true symphony – so noble, pure, and richly unified – by substituting in its place the brilliant caprices of his musical imagination"; he was "more a friend of the extraordinary than he was respectful of the consecrated form" of the "admirable" symphonic genre.[10] Thus it was that as a composer of dramatic instrumental music Berlioz found it necessary to become the independent impresario and self-supporting concert manager who put on the performances of his first two symphonies himself, as we have observed, and who put on hundreds of further concerts over the next thirty-five years. He developed his skills as a conductor, he experimented with the spatial disposition of the orchestra, he invented the time- and money-saving device of the sectional rehearsal, and he facilitated the full dress rehearsal by fixing rehearsal letters – a novel idea at the time – to his scores and parts.

In the previous chapter I mentioned some of the concerts that Berlioz organized in the eighteen-twenties to make himself known to the Parisian public and to increase his chances of winning the Prix de Rome; and we have just heard of some of the concerts he gave after returning from Rome, as he opened a struggle to win a place in the French musical establishment and at the same time to shape it to his own standards of excellence. Each of the major performances of Berlioz's works is in fact a story in itself. None is typical, for unlike the offerings of the Société des Concerts, Berlioz's featured a varied repertory, changing singers and instrumentalists, a number of more or less suitable concert halls, and a diverse, non-subscription public. (To establish the complete programs of these concerts is no easy task, for Berlioz and other writers at the time were far more casual than we are about names of performers and titles of works.) Near the center of his most fertile decade, in the autumn of 1836, Berlioz gave two concerts that may serve as further illustrations of his procedure.

On 4 December 1836, having obtained the Salle du Conservatoire (as he had been able regularly to do, on a limited basis, since 1832), Berlioz gave a program that consisted of five works: (1) *Harold en Italie*, in its entirety, with Chrétien Urhan as viola soloist (as he had been at the première of the work in 1834); (2) *Fête martiale en Écosse*, a solo for harp composed and performed by Théodore Labarre; (3) *Une Larme*, a setting by Urhan of a poem by Alphonse de Lamartine, for soprano, violin, and cello, performed by Cornélie Falcon, Urhan, and Pierre-Alexandre Chevillard; (4) Quasimodo's *Air des cloches* from Louise Bertin's opera *Esméralda* (premiered at the Opéra three weeks earlier, on 14 November), sung by Auguste Massol; (5) *Épisode de la vie d'un artiste* – the *Symphonie fantastique*, that is, performed in its entirety.

On 18 December, in the same hall, he was joined by Franz Liszt in giving a program that consisted of nine works: (1) *Grande Ouverture des Francs-Juges*; (2) an aria by Saverio Mercadante, sung by the bass Louis Alizard (who, at twenty-one, was the recent winner of a *premier prix de chant* at the Conservatoire); (3) *Grande Fantaisie symphonique, avec piano principal, sur deux thèmes du Mélologue de M. Berlioz* – the work for piano and orchestra that Liszt wrote for this occasion on themes from *Le Pêcheur* and the *Chanson de brigands* of *Le Retour à la vie*; (4) *L'Ange et l'enfant*, a song for soprano and orchestra by Urhan, sung by Maria Nau,

who had made her début at the Opéra nine months earlier at the première of Meyerbeer's *Les Huguenots*; (5) a solo for unaccompanied
cello, composed and performed by the principal cellist of the
Hamburg Opera, Sebastien Lee, then on tour in Paris; (6) *Divertissement*
for solo piano, composed by Liszt on the cavatina *I tuoi frequente palpiti*
from Giovanni Pacini's opera *Niobe* of 1826; (7) an aria from Bellini's
La Sonnambula sung by Maria Nau; (8) *Le Bal* and the *Marche au supplice*
from the *Symphonie fantastique*, played by Liszt, who had completed a
solo piano transcription of the symphony in the summer of 1833; (9)
the first two movements of *Harold en Italie*, with Urhan as viola soloist.

The varied items and sound combinations here suggest a lesson to
those who would achieve "authenticity" in presenting the music of the
past, for to put on this sort of immense program now would surely
communicate above all the feeling of nineteenth-century *time* (while
merely using old instruments guarantees nothing). It is a sign of how
consumed Berlioz was with preparing these concerts – rehearsing the
players, priming the press – that no letters of his are preserved from
early November until late December of 1836. On the 22nd of that
month, Berlioz finally reported to his sister Adèle on his activities in a
long and leisurely letter, which opens in a way that is highly characteristic of Berlioz's post-concert comments:

> I have just given two concerts. In terms of art, I have never had such a
> great success, because of the immensely superior results I achieved
> by conducting the orchestra myself. In terms of money, because the
> expenses of each concert came to 1,800 francs and because the
> proceeds of the second had to be shared with Liszt, I made a net profit
> of 1,600 francs; I am further owed 160 francs for tickets I put on sale
> in town, and 64 francs for the loge of the Minister of the Interior, who
> came to the first concert but who, I am sure, will never pay for it.
> Assuming this to be the case, I will therefore have made 1,760 francs
> in two weeks – a sum I urgently needed to pay the bills at the furniture
> store and other charges on which payment is now due.

In the following paragraph Berlioz complains about the meagre
profits, reduced because he had to offer so many free tickets to the

press, then crows about the overwhelmingly favorable reviews of the concert that appeared in all the newspapers, which he lists in detail. He does not mention that after the second concert, Meyerbeer shook his hand and offered such hearty congratulations that George Sand, also in attendance, said she would never forget such a genuine demonstration of warmth.[11]

At this moment in his career, then, apart from financial worries – which he not infrequently mentions in the same breath as his artistic gains and losses – Berlioz was optimistic about his professional situation as he gradually approached the long-awaited goal of all his training and experience as a composer, the bringing of major work to the stage of the Académie Royale de Musique. At the same time he was nearly exhausted by his other activities, most particularly his journalism – for almost in spite of himself, Berlioz was becoming a newspaperman, and his career as a critic, ever more time-consuming, was beginning to blossom.

Superbly prepared for the task, with a broadly inquisitive intellect and a rapier wit, Berlioz had begun with enthusiasm to make contributions to the press, under the impression that this could be a temporary means of supplementing his income while educating the public to new ways of thinking about music. But by 1837 he had a secure position at the leading Orleanist newspaper, the Journal des débats, where he succeeded François-Henri-Joseph Blaze – known by his pseudonym, Castil-Blaze – as chief music critic. (Berlioz long denigrated Castil-Blaze's popularizations of well-known operas, but he profited from the older man's distinctive accomplishments in raising the standards of writing about music in the press.) Berlioz had also become the leading reviewer for Maurice Schlesinger's Revue et Gazette musicale; and he was "besieged," as he told his father, by offers from a host of other journals as well. Berlioz never thought that a life of prose was la vie en rose, but he often expressed bitter resentment at having to write criticism, as what was supplementary became permanent, and as what he wanted to write was supplanted by what he had to write. The relief he

7 This *portrait-charge* of Berlioz, *ca.* 1836, was made by the creator of the
   caricature-statuette, Jean-Pierre Dantan, known as Dantan *jeune*. The rebus
   (*Ber-lit-haut*) suggests that the z of the composer's name could be silent.

expressed on retiring from journalism in 1863, after a career that had spanned nearly forty years, rings true.

And yet the wisdom and humor of so many of Berlioz's articles – of which fewer than a quarter are familiar from the later collections he brought out as *Les Soirées de l'orchestre* (1852), *Les Grotesques de la musique* (1859), and *A Travers chants* (1862) – simply cannot be the product of a soul constantly in torment. (Even after his "retirement," for example, Berlioz contributed an occasional *boutade* to the *Revue et Gazette musicale*.)[12] If Berlioz viewed the art of the composer as more noble than the craft of the critic, and minimized the value of his journalism, which allowed too little time for other creative work, the biographer need not and ought not to take over his prejudice in this regard, for underlining the importance of his writing in no way undermines the importance of his music.

On rare occasion, the external pressure of camaraderie or politics led Berlioz to accentuate the positive or circumvent the negative in a particular column, at which time he would tell friends not to believe a word of what he had written. But for the most part, his reviews – effusions, polemics, literary fantasies – were set down with the same conviction as were his scores. The powerful sword he wielded as a critic thus became a double-edged one, as writing on principle – "I can no more not admire a sublime work by my greatest foe than not detest a frightful nonsense by my dearest friend," he told the Princess Wittgenstein, years later, in 1864 – gained him considerably more enemies than allies.

Of the many ideas Berlioz expressed in his critical writings, it is possible to give no sweet and lucid distillation. Still, the opening of one of Berlioz's first articles is instructive as to what underlies much of his criticism in the eighteen-thirties and beyond. In an "Aperçu sur la musique classique et la musique romantique," Berlioz – like E. T. A. Hoffmann, whose writings did so much to define a new, "romantic" era – equated heart-felt and deeply emotional music with "romanticism," and went on to suggest a succinct definition of music itself –

which is, of all the arts, the one that is most fundamentally free, and
the one that has been for the longest time under the yoke of prejudice
and dogmatism. [...] Music is the art of moving by means of sounds
those who are sensitive, intelligent, educated, and blessed with
imagination. It is addressed uniquely to them, and this is why it is not
meant for everyone.

These words appeared in the magazine Le Correspondant on 22 October
1830, shortly after Berlioz's victory in the Prix de Rome competition
and seven weeks before the première of the Symphonie fantastique. He
used the same definition in "De la musique en général," published
now, in the Revue et Gazette musicale, in 1837; he used it again, in a
Dictionnaire de la conversation that appeared in the same year; he used it
in his first collection of essays (the Voyage musical en Allemagne of 1844),
and he used it at the opening of his last (A Travers chants of 1862). In the
later versions, Berlioz removed the marks of writing from his prose:

Music: the art of moving by combinations of sound intelligent men
gifted with special and practiced sense organs. To define music in
this way is to avow that we do not believe that it is, as is often said,
made for everyone.

Music is not made for tout le monde – the expression he used in 1830
and (set off in italics) reused for more than thirty years. This was not
mere emphasis, it was polemic, for in offering a definition of music –
not really necessary for his readers, after all – Berlioz was in fact
making sport of La Musique mise à la portée de tout le monde – "Music
explained to the world," one might say, or "Music made easy" – the
title of a then popular handbook by the professor at the Conservatoire
who was the editor of the Revue Musicale (and of the Beethoven
Symphonies, with emendations that Berlioz reproached), François-
Joseph Fétis. The handbook had appeared at the beginning of 1830
and was often reprinted and translated into at least five foreign languages. Its subtitle – "a succinct account of everything necessary to
judge and to speak about this art without having studied it" – was the
subject of some ridicule, though in fact Fétis, here as the inventor of

"music appreciation" and elsewhere as a broad-minded historian and a far-sighted theorist, was an intelligent and forceful advocate of music both old and new.

It is a sign of Berlioz's youthful audaciousness that he took on Fétis at the beginning of his journalistic career. For some two decades the older figure, who became the founding director of the Conservatoire in Brussels in 1833 and the author of the most important biographical dictionary of the century, lashed out at the younger composer with charges – such as that Berlioz was not a true musician – which tended to take on wide currency. (Rossini owes to Fétis his reputation for laziness, for example, which modern scholars still feel constrained to refute.) Berlioz's uncompromising attitude about the importance of artful listeners for artful music, in itself highly admirable, was something that failed to endear him to the broader musical public, and the theme of the privileged few – artists, writers, reflective persons of many occupations, the "brains" of Paris, as Balzac might have called them – runs through a host of his writings for the press. Berlioz must have realized that to denigrate the audience was to risk biting the hand that fed him. But he no more believed in the eventual good sense of the broad general public, in the arena of the arts, than he believed in universal suffrage, in the arena of the law.

The most renowned critic of Berlioz's day, Sainte-Beuve, made it a principle to study an author in order to apprehend his work. This "scientific" method was challenged by Marcel Proust in a celebrated collection of essays, where it is suggested that the "I" who creates art is different from the "I" who eats, sleeps, and drinks like everyone else. Challenging the relevance of personal and biographical information to the act of interpretation became the stuff of much critical writing in the twentieth century; but in the bottle of the now outmoded "new criticism," some of the wine was very old indeed. If we were to take his several reviews of the score of *Les Huguenots* as exemplary of his procedures, for example – Meyerbeer's opera became the greatest operatic success of the century, and Berlioz wrote about it in both the *Revue et Gazette musicale* and the *Journal des débats*, we would see that Berlioz explicitly dissociated himself from those who explained art via biography, and that he went through the score in a manner which can reasonably be called objective, exploring the music uniquely in terms of its advancement or enhancement of the drama.

Had Berlioz the critic been confronted primarily by the works of Beethoven – his usual beat at the *Revue et Gazette musicale* was the Conservatoire, where Beethoven was the main item on the menu of the Société des Concerts – we might find it difficult to understand why he found journalism so tedious. But his usual fare at the *Débats* consisted of ballets and opéras comiques by figures now seen to be of the second or third rank, such as Boisselot, Caraffa, Clapisson, Gomis, Mainzer, and Reber, to name but a few. After looking at the complete list of works that Berlioz reviewed, one better understands the special respect he sensed for the construction and lyricism of Cherubini, Rossini, and Meyerbeer, the genuine admiration he felt for the learning and imagination of Mendelssohn, and the awe he experienced in the face of the dramatic truths evoked by Beethoven and Gluck.

Was Berlioz ever grateful for the opportunity journalism allowed him to speak to a wide audience – something much appreciated by those who used the métier as a stepping stone to a career in politics? Was he ever pleased by the chance to lecture to others about his own high regard for the art as he believed it ought to be practiced? Was he happy to be associated at the *Débats* with a group of progressive writers and critics of considerable distinction and influence, working for a newspaper with a circulation of well over ten thousand, and a readership of intelligence and broad general culture? Of this there is little evidence, for the only advantages he mentions, regarding journalism, were those of the pocketbook (and even these were slim). The going rate at the *Journal des débats* for an eight-column *feuilleton* – a spread at the bottom of the first page of the newspaper that often ran over to page 2 – was one hundred francs: this equaled Berlioz's entire monthly income in his student days, and it equaled the monthly salary of a low-level government employee in the eighteen-twenties and thirties. When he wrote for the *Revue et Gazette musicale*, he was less well paid, but he enjoyed a readership of considerable musical instruction. The series of articles that he published there under the rubric of "De l'Instrumentation," for example, between 21 November 1841 and 17 July 1842, formed the substance of his first book, the technically demanding *Grand Traité d'instrumentation et d'orchestration modernes* (printed in December 1843 and released a few months later). Here, guided by the writings of his former teacher, Antonin Reicha, and of his friend, Georges Kastner, Berlioz demonstrated the intricate properties of the orchestral instruments and the niceties of orchestral technique at a time when instrument manufacture was in a stage of rapid and imaginative development; and he demonstrated the ear for accent and timbre that long informed his composing and conducting alike. The learning incorporated into the orchestration treatise was passed on to generations of future composers, and lives on to this day as a central element of Berlioz's artistic legacy.

Criticism is a form of autobiography, Oscar Wilde is credited with having said, and to this rule Berlioz presents no exception. From the partial selection of his criticism that has been long available we know that Berlioz was fiercely independent; that he was preoccupied with the dramatic motivation of music both operatic and instrumental; that he distinguished between those of average ability who listened with indifference and those of superior discrimination who listened with the sort of fierce concentration he espoused; that he was cool to most of the music of his contemporaries; and that while he never truly warmed to the music of the greatest modernists of the day, Liszt and Wagner, he committed no gaffe so gross as that of the writer for *Le Figaro*, who read *Madame Bovary* and proclaimed that "Monsieur Flaubert is not a writer"; or so great as that of the editor of the *Revue Musicale*, who heard the *Épisode de la vie d'un artiste* and proclaimed that "Monsieur Berlioz is not a musician." When we are able to read his collected criticism from cover to cover – at which point a *new* biography of Berlioz will be called for – we will know more about the doings of his daily life as he tramped from theater to theater to review concerts and operas, grand and frivolous, and about the true extent of his patience and wisdom. That he always found something colorful to write about, whether the subject to hand proved to be vivid or dull, suggests that his actual feelings about journalism were not mono-chromatic, but variable, and mixed.

Commissions for the nation

For the first five years of the rule of Louis-Philippe, it was fair to say that "the King reigns but does not govern"; certainly the press was more free from government interference and thus more flourishing than ever before. Only after Giuseppe Fieschi's attempt on Louis-Philippe's life, on 28 July 1835, were the so-called "September Laws" passed, which required entertainments of all sorts to receive pre-liminary authorization from the Ministry of the Interior. (Fieschi's explosion caused the death of some forty members of the National Guard, and Berlioz, like everyone else, was shocked by the event.) The régime of Louis-Philippe then became a modified extension of the constitutional monarchy of the Bourbon Restoration and an attempt to maintain in equilibrium the forces of the extremes in some sort of *juste milieu* or "golden mean." But Charles X's last-ditch attempt to bring glory upon his reign by sending the army to conquer Algiers had consequences that reverberated throughout the July Monarchy: the Duc d'Orléans and the other Princes of the Blood (Nemours, Montpensier, Aumale) with whom Berlioz also had regular contact – their preceptor, Alfred-Auguste Cuvillier-Fleury, was Berlioz's col-league at the *Débats* – were long involved in the drawn out and painful Algerian War. The Duc de Montpensier became the dedicatee of Berlioz's book-length account of his foreign travels, the *Voyage musical en Allemagne*, and the composer later spoke of him, in 1846, as a man of "noble spirit, good heart, and full of ardent enthusiasm for everything that concerned the well-being of the art of music." (At that time Montpensier was attempting to have the Minister of War commission Berlioz to write a symphony with a chorus of three thousand men, on the theme of *Le Retour de l'armée d'Italie* – the return of Napoleon's army from the great Italian conquests, that is, which were formalized by the signing of the Treaty of Campo Formio in 1797 – but the project never came to fruition.)

It was the Duc d'Aumale (also an occasional auditor at Berlioz's concerts), who finally accepted the surrender of the Algerian warlords at the end of 1847, not long before the demise of the Orléans régime. But it was the death of a General, in 1837, at the taking of the citadel of Constantine, that had especial consequences for Berlioz's career.

About Mozart's last work, a well-known scholar once wrote an article entitled "Requiem but no peace."[13] Such words fit the story that Berlioz tells of his own *Requiem*, the *Grande Messe des morts*, which was commissioned in the spring of 1837 by the Minister of the Interior, the Comte Adrien de Gasparin, to mark the anniversary of the death of Maréchal Édouard Mortier, the much decorated former War Minister, who was among those killed on 28 July 1835 when the Corsican Fieschi's primitive bomb went off. Gasparin's plan was to have a Requiem Mass performed on the appropriate day at the Église des Invalides, not only in honor of Mortier and the others killed in the attack, but also in honor of the heroes of the July Revolution of five years earlier. That he turned to Berlioz for the commission, when Cherubini, with the newly completed D minor Requiem in his portfolio, was the more obvious beneficiary, is a sure sign of the good favor that Berlioz enjoyed in high places, and of the reputation he must already have had as a patriotic composer with a penchant and a talent for the musically grandiose.

Shortly after his interview with the Minister, on 8 March 1837, the composer hastened to prepare the new work, taking over the *Resurrexit* of the *Messe solennelle* of 1824 and shaping it into the nucleus of a colossal *Requiem* that exemplifies at once the enormity of the Last Judgment and the limits of Berlioz's sonic imagination. Berlioz echoed the grandeur of this *Dies irae* in the *Rex tremendae* and the *Lacrimosa*, interweaving among these three grandiloquent statements movements of a more tranquil and reflective tone. He opened with a quiet *Introit* (whose several expanding statements recall the beginning of Cherubini's C minor *Requiem* – was Berlioz practicing one-upmanship?), and he closed with an *Agnus Dei* that recapitulates parts of the *Kyrie* and the *Hostias* and in so doing lends to the larger composition a satisfyingly circular character which suggests a vision of eternal rest. From the start, Berlioz's conception, informed by the spirit of the communal rites of thanksgiving of the period of the Great Revolution of 1789 (and probably by the pre-revolutionary *Requiem* of François-Joseph Gossec), was essentially a dramatic one, whose centerpiece can be likened to a musical clenched fist raised heavenward in a gesture of defiance at *le dernier jour du monde* (the title he applied to a series of monumental projects he imagined but did not realize in the earlier eighteen-thirties).

The first musical thought that Berlioz had when the Minister broached the subject – "quel *Dies irae!!!*" – remains the last thought of many listeners to the *Requiem*, and, misleadingly, I am afraid, to Berlioz's œuvre as a whole. Still, the disposition of the orchestra, at the *Tuba mirum*, is staggering, as four separate brass ensembles sound the alarm from their places at the four corners of the main choral and orchestral space (Gossec, too, used an "orchestre éloigné" at this point): entering in a sequential pattern from west to east, then north to south, the brass build a harmonic and rhythmic crescendo that is capped by a tremendous noise from eight pairs of timpani and two bass drums. Fanfare at this moment is a tradition of the Requiem Mass, but Berlioz's furious gesture – fitted to the sonorous chapel of the Invalides, before Napoleon's tomb became its centerpiece – outstrips everything that had gone before. "Many fail to recognize," Berlioz wrote in *Le Rénovateur* not quite two years earlier, on 19 July 1835,

> that the very building in which music is made is itself a musical
> instrument, that it is to the performers what the sound board is to
> the strings of the violin, viola, cello, bass, harp, and piano stretched
> above. A correlation between the size and interior shape of the edifice
> and the number of performers is thus an absolute necessity.

Here we have an explanation of the sounds and of the *silences between the sounds* that may be found in the *Requiem* and others of Berlioz's large-scale compositions. The conception of music as a counterpoint of sound and silence was not original to Berlioz – Haydn told jokes with it, Beethoven struck thunderbolts – but his concern for acoustics can explain aspects of his music that may otherwise seem peculiar indeed.

Berlioz completed the score of the *Requiem* at the end of June 1837, and was then abruptly informed – after having gone to the considerable expense of having the parts copied by professionals – that the memorial ceremony, in a budget-cutting move, was going to take place without music. For months he had to do battle with the administration for the promised compensation of four thousand francs (plus an even greater amount to pay the copyists), and gained partial satisfaction only when chance caused the performance to be rescheduled. On 11 October, the commanding General of the French forces in North Africa, the Comte Charles-Denys de Damrémont, was killed during the taking of Constantine, the oldest city in Algeria and the foothold of the future French domination of North Africa. Berlioz adroitly proposed to have his *Requiem* performed at the Invalides in honor of the slain officer, and his proposal was accepted by the Minister of War.

For some who reviewed the performance that now took place, on 5 December 1837, Berlioz's triumph was as grand as the taking of Constantine itself. Even the delayed payment for his work (which finally arrived in February of the new year) did not darken Berlioz's post-concert spirits: this was the "greatest and most difficultly achieved success of his career"; it left him full of hope and possibility, and proud of a work which, as he told his mother, was likely to become "the property of the nation."[14] Now, the "nation" was overwhelmingly Catholic, of course, while the lasting impression made by Berlioz's work seems more theatrical than religious. The nature of Berlioz's faith is not easily explained, for one must account for the fact that he composed this work and others in the category of sacred music, yet irreverently announced on the first page of the *Mémoires* that he had long since taken leave of the Catholic Church. What one can say without controversy is that the *Requiem* has become a symbol –

like the tri-colored flag, and the Panthéon – of the one church of which Berlioz was a more than sometimes member, and that is the common church of flamboyance, or of what one might want to call "Frenchness" itself.

Berlioz's account of the genesis and performance of the *Requiem*, in chapter 46 of the *Mémoires*, mentions an incredible and amusing event whose veracity (since it is nowhere mentioned in his correspondence of the time) is clearly open to question. Writing in the eighteen-fifties of what took place in 1837, he asserts that at the most important moment of the entire work – when the tempo broadens from the Moderato of the *Dies irae* to the Andante maestoso of the *Tuba mirum*, when the supplementary brass choirs enter with a quadraphonic fanfare – the conductor, Habeneck, intentionally put down his baton, reached for his tobacco pouch, and took a pinch of snuff (causing Berlioz to jump up, give the new tempo himself, and thereby avoid catastrophe). Rehearsing this incident in his translation of the *Mémoires*, David Cairns notes that of all places in the *Requiem*, this one is "the most unlikely for snuff-taking if the conductor is merely negligent, the most likely if he is actuated by malice." It is also the most likely place to select, of course, if one wants to construct a sardonic tale of incompetence and revenge: particularly after emerging as a professional conductor in his own right, Berlioz had doubts about Habeneck's ability and for some years resented his official authority. It was probably for this reason that Berlioz invented the incident, knowing that it would cause a ruckus. But he may have based his fiction upon a true recollection – of something *twice* mentioned in letters contemporary with the performance – that at this sensational moment one of the members of the *chorus* was overcome by nervous excitement. To restore him, perhaps they administered snuff.[15]

In July 1837, Berlioz was a potential candidate for a civil-service post, the first of many such might-have-beens in his career, when the Minister of Public Instruction, the Comte de Salvandy, considered authorizing him to supervise the teaching of music as Inspecteur général de l'enseignement musical. Inspectors of this sort were becoming gradually more common in the aftermath of the Guizot Law of 28 June 1833, which attempted to ensure nationwide norms for an educational system that varied widely in quality from one province to the next. (National educational standards became one of the great legacies of the Third French Republic.) In 1837, however, the appointment for Berlioz did not come to pass. Nor did it in 1842, when, after the death of Guillaume-Louis Bocquillon Wilhem (on 28 April), the Duc d'Orléans, Armand Bertin of the *Journal des débats*, and François Guizot himself, the most powerful voice in the Chambre des Députés, recommended that Berlioz accede to Wilhem's post of Inspecteur du chant in the primary schools of Paris. As founder of the Orphéon, the choral-singing movement in France, Wilhem was a pioneer in the musical education of the young, and had developed a system of ear-training and sight-reading that, most writers seem to agree, was highly efficacious. Despite such high-level support, however, the Municipal Council of Paris preferred to give a field promotion to Wilhem's little-known assistant, the singer Joseph Hubert. Berlioz was usually skeptical of new-fangled systems of musical instruction, of course, and had he had the opportunity to play a role in the educational administration of his day, he would probably have had youngsters copying out the works of Gluck.

Berlioz had another rendezvous with administrative politics in the opening six months of 1838, in the aftermath of the successful première of the *Requiem*, when he attempted to obtain the privilege of directing one of the principal theaters of the capital, the Théâtre Italien, where Parisians of the eighteen-twenties and thirties first heard the works of Rossini, Bellini, and Donizetti in surroundings even more sumptuous than those of the Opéra. Here was an office that would have provided Berlioz with a fixed annual salary of ten thousand francs and a percentage of this fashionable theater's revenues such that, were he to make a success of the venture, he would become a wealthy man indeed. All of Berlioz's modern biographers have minimized his efforts to obtain the directorship of the "Italiens," as it was called, finding the composer an unlikely candidate for a post more associated with business than with art. But after the great fire at the theater in January 1838, which led to the death of one of the current co-directors and the injury of the other, Berlioz formed a bona fide association with a composer-colleague, Henri de Ruolz (Henri-Catherine-Camille Comte de Ruolz-Montchal, that is), and with some wealthy businessmen associated with the powerful Bertin family, owners of the *Journal des débats*, and he attempted assiduously to gain this special foothold in the city's artistic world.

The strategy of "Berlioz and Company," as the enterprise was styled, was to rebuild the burnt-out Salle Favart and to ask for no government subsidy, something that would reduce the administration's expenditures on the arts by the considerable sum of at least seventy thousand francs and thus please those whose incipient capitalist mentality viewed such privatization as progress. After meeting with the commissioners who oversaw the operatic theaters, and with the Comte de Montalivet, Minister of the Interior, Berlioz actually signed the contract, on 4 June 1838, that would give him the directorship of the Théâtre Italien. On the same day the King himself signed the bill that would legalize the transaction, leading the *Revue et Gazette musicale* to report (on 10 June) that "the directorship of the Théâtre Italien has just been offered, for fifteen years, to M. Berlioz, our collaborator." The bill had to be approved by the legislature, however, and to the Minister's surprise and chagrin, it was voted down: the plans were too vague, the arrangements with the new managers too generous, and the commissioners, in assuming the authority to dispose of the theater as they wished, too hasty.

The real rebuke was to the Bertins, who were popularly accused of wanting to purchase a theater for their protégé (Berlioz), and even more for Louise Bertin, who had already had an opera, *Fausto*, performed at the Théâtre Italien, but with little success, in 1831. In June 1838 Berlioz was too preoccupied with *Benvenuto Cellini*, at the Opéra, to have felt the effects of this rejection by the Chambre des Députés –

whose action, contrary to the will of the King, offers proof of the new-found strength of that legislative body – and he makes almost nothing of it in his correspondence of the time. But I should like to think that he would have made a fine imprint on Parisian musical life as director of the theater, for the skills that would have been entailed – contracting, commissioning, casting, calculating, and, one must suppose, conducting – were hardly foreign to a man who would make a career as a self-employed concert producer and impresario. The case of Cherubini at the Conservatoire, while not entirely analogous, none the less clearly demonstrates that a great creator can be a great administrator as well.

The indispensable mark of achievement of a composer in France in the nineteenth century was a triumph at the government-supported Opéra, and some of those who made the Revolution of 1830 thought that Prix de Rome winners ought *automatically* to be granted the privilege of composing a work for the nation's most exalted theater (just as painters and sculptors were routinely commissioned to produce statues, fountains, murals, and busts for the nation's majestic monuments and public buildings). But when Émile Lubbert was replaced at the helm of the Opéra by a businessman, Louis-Désiré Véron, who was charged with bringing to all productions a "pomp and luxury" appropriate to the national theater, then the institution became more of a commercial enterprise than ever before, and musical works were commissioned and sustained in proportion to their promise of financial success. Meyerbeer's *Robert le diable* led the way: its satanic characters and gothic ruins, its brilliant cast and striking orchestral colors led to a hundred performances in only three years. (Berlioz, in Italy in November 1831, was chagrined to have missed the première.) Still, the machinations that eventually led to the acceptance at the Opéra of his own *Benvenuto Cellini* were not entirely divorced from the earlier, less mercantile mentality, for, as the Duc de Choiseul wrote in 1835, when he was in charge of the Special Commission that oversaw the royal theaters, "the success already achieved by M. Berlioz and his capacity as a laureate of the Conservatoire gives him the right to the encouragement of the administration."[16]

Berlioz and others always spoke of the Académie Royale de Musique (the Opéra) as a kind of monarchy, substituting for the King the name of the director and speaking of the "administration Véron" or the "administration Pillet." It seems to have been an understood precondition of his contract with the government that when the architect Edmond Duponchel succeeded Louis Véron as director of the Opéra, in August 1835, he would engage Berlioz to compose the first opera of his régime. A satirical journal of the day suggested that Berlioz was *imposed* upon the administration of the theater "by order of the Ministry of the Interior and by the Chancellery of His Majesty King Bertin I" – Louis Bertin, that is, owner of the *Journal des débats*.[17] Be this as it may (the full story is marked by intrigue as political as it was artistic), the work that came into being – on a libretto by the major figures Auguste Barbier and Alfred de Vigny and the minor figure Léon de Wailly – was *Benvenuto Cellini*, an opera based in part on episodes from the life of the Italian artist born at the dawn of the sixteenth century, and in part on a droll story, *Signor Formica*, by E. T. A. Hoffmann. With its rapid-fire choruses and frequent metrical displacements, the work was of a difficulty considerably greater than that of the works by Rossini, Meyerbeer, Auber, and Halévy that dominated the repertory at the time (*Guillaume Tell*, *Robert le diable*, *Gustave III*, *La Juive*), and with its few opportunities for soloistic display, it was of a sobriety to disappoint amateurs of ornate vocal lyricism. (The Cellini, Gilbert Duprez, had become king of the tenors in 1837, when he assumed the role of Arnold in Rossini's *Guillaume Tell*. It was he who sang the solo part in the *Sanctus* of the *Requiem*, in December of that year.) Further, with its mixture of satire and seriousness and especially its occasional use of frankly crude expressions in a house that normally required the elegant circumlocutions of the well-made libretto, the opera was found to be shocking by many critics who, lacking musical sophistication, judged opera entirely on the basis of the words they read and heard.

Benvenuto Cellini had three complete performances in September 1838, one in January 1839, and three further partial performances in the spring of that year. The work was then withdrawn by the composer, and sentenced to a career that has remained checkered to this day. No work of Berlioz's is more in need of brilliant modern performance than this, in a version that restores the cuts made in the eighteen-fifties for performances in Weimar and London (which among other things reduce the comic elements that are, I think, intrinsic to the original conception) and that resembles what was performed in Paris, in 1838, during the second week of September.

In the summer of 1843 Berlioz refashioned two passages from the opera – the Andante sung by Cellini and Teresa in the First Tableau, and the Prestissimo double chorus in the Second – into the *Ouverture du Carnaval romain*. This brilliantly scored work became a frequent and useful item on Berlioz's concert programs for over twenty-five years. He called it an *ouverture caractéristique*, presumably because of its colorful evocation of the carnival spirit. But it is characteristic, too, of others of his concert overtures that have become staples of the modern repertory, as conductors from Harty and Beecham to Bernstein and beyond have brought them energetically to life. Like the overture to the opera *Béatrice et Bénédict* (as well as that of *Benvenuto Cellini* itself), and like the overture *Le Corsaire* of 1844, *Le Carnaval romain* compounds slow and fast tempos and opposing emotions in ways that are simple yet highly exciting.

For much of the eighteen-twenties, one of Berlioz's second homes in Paris was the reading room of the library at the Conservatoire, where he enjoyed the privilege of using a collection that was *publique et ouverte* since the foundation of the school in 1795, and where he studied and copied scores by Beethoven and Gluck. We can be sure, from the *Mémoires'* hilarious account of Berlioz's first encounter with Cherubini, that the officious director was well aware of Berlioz's passion for that particular locale. Is this why Cherubini wrote to the Minister of the Interior, on 2 January 1838, to propose that Berlioz be given a post there? It is at any rate not without poetic justice that, one year later, on 9 January 1839, Berlioz was awarded his first official position, at the Conservatoire, as Conservateur adjoint in the library. There he served the head librarian, Auguste Bottée de Toulmon, by handling a number of largely secretarial matters that consumed little time and no creative energy. Still, political plum though the position might have been, whenever Berlioz prepared to leave Paris to go on tour, he had always to ask the director for permission to take an extended leave. Cherubini's successor at the Conservatoire, Daniel-François-Esprit Auber, was always willing to grant such leaves without objection and with pay. Indeed, the coincidence of the beginning of Berlioz's career as a traveling conductor and of Auber's as director of the Conservatoire, in 1842, suggests that Cherubini may not have favored his assistant librarian with so many paid leaves of absence. But Auber, who had been on good terms with Berlioz since at least 1829, was also a stickler for protocol: even as an elder statesman of French music, when he was invited to visit Russia by the Grand Duchess Yelena Pavlovna, Berlioz had to write to Auber, in the autumn of 1867, saying that "I cannot go without your permission."[18]

Let it be remembered that a number of prominent nineteenth-century writers at one time or another held library positions of some sort, including Victor Hugo, Sainte-Beuve, Charles Nodier, Alfred de Musset, Gustave Flaubert, Prosper Mérimée, and Alexandre Dumas, who was briefly librarian for the Duc d'Orléans. Historians have written of the lackadaisical manner in which Berlioz took his responsibilities at the library, and since some of these historians were themselves librarians at the Conservatoire, one can well understand their irritation. But one ought not to lose sight of the forest for the trees, for it was surely a progressive act in the early capitalist era for the administration to have offered such dull sinecures to artists whose primary work was less certainly remunerated, and who, in the light of history, have become bright stars indeed.

Bibliothécaire du Conservatoire was thus a perfectly honorable title in a French cultural world where titles, then as now, carried considerable prestige. But the title of Professeur would have suited Berlioz better. His first chance at it came in 1838, when Étienne Rifault, professor of harmony, died in March of that year. Berlioz submitted his candidacy for the post to Cherubini, but withdrew it "of his own accord," according to the minutes of the search committee, "when he learned that in addition to the teaching of harmony the post required the teaching of accompaniment as well – something [Berlioz] would be unable to do, since he does not play the piano."[19] Rifault had indeed been a pianist, but the man chosen in preference to Berlioz, Paul-Émile Bienaimé, was himself primarily a singer, with little or no keyboard experience – suggesting that Cherubini and the other voting members of the staff (the composers Berton and Paër, the violinist-conductor Habeneck, and five instrumental teachers) simply preferred to hire one of their own: Bienaimé had been teaching solfège at the school for some years, and had on occasion replaced the ailing Rifault.

The "old-boy network" prevailed again in 1839, when Paër was succeeded as professor of composition not by Berlioz (who once more proposed his candidacy to Cherubini, on 10 May of that year), but by the Neapolitan composer Michele-Enrico Carafa. Four years later, on 26 February 1844, Berlioz finally took the bull by the horns and wrote an urgent letter to the then Minister of the Interior, the Comte Duchatel, with the request that he create a *new* class at the Conservatoire, in instrumentation, for which Berlioz, as the author of the newly completed treatise on the subject, was uniquely equipped. But the entreaty, which poignantly lamented how much of his day was consumed by journalism ("I am a composer but I have no time to compose"), went unfulfilled.

A composition to celebrate the fifth anniversary of the July Revolution may have occurred to Berlioz as early as the summer of 1835, when he drafted two movements of a work he called a *Fête musicale funèbre à la*

8 Eugène Formentin's lithograph of Berlioz, *ca.* 1839. Despite the image, Berlioz presumably conducted with the baton in his right hand.

mémoire des hommes illustres de la France. (Like Beethoven, Berlioz, too, was captivated by the theme of the death of the hero.) The *Fête* was never completed, but those two movements may have been used in one of the two grand works that Berlioz did complete in response to explicit commissions from the French government: the *Requiem* of 1837, and the *Funeral and Triumphal Symphony* of 1840.

On the occasion of the tenth anniversary of the Revolution of 1830, at which time the great column of the Bastille was inaugurated and the remains of the original victims were translated "to the vast tomb below" (as Berlioz noted in a letter), the new Minister of the Interior, Charles de Rémusat, a true "friend of music," commissioned Berlioz to write what became the *Symphonie funèbre et triomphale*. This ceremonial work – two march movements enclosing a central funeral oration that is "declaimed" by a solo trombone – was designed for large military band. And it was designed for execution out-of-doors, even though Berlioz usually found such open-air occasions more "pompous mystifications" than anything else. On the anniversary day of 28 July 1840, a uniformed Berlioz (marching backwards) led his two-hundred-man musical army from the Place de la Concorde to the Place de la Bastille, playing the new work repeatedly, to great applause, and, soon thereafter, to great critical acclaim.

Among the admirers of the symphony was Rémusat himself, whose father had been superintendent of theaters under Napoleon I, and who was something of a musical amateur. Having read Berlioz's *Mémoires* by the time he composed his own, the ex-Minister gives an account of the occasion that is rather more cool than the composer's:

> Berlioz was a highly spirited man whom some of my friends considered a musician of great genius. In his *Mémoires*, published posthumously, he recites the whole story of the [*Symphonie funèbre*], which he considered very important, and he embellishes his recitation with anecdotes that redound to my honor, even though we had in fact no personal acquaintance. Because he believed himself justified, from earlier experience, in complaining about the offices

of the Ministry of the Interior, he determined to sing my praises. So if Berlioz's *Mémoires* are read in the future, I will be remembered, without meriting the compliment, as the Minister who most loved music and who best treated musicians.

This may be false modesty on Rémusat's part; for Berlioz to have called him "un ami de la musique" and a "gentleman" is rare indeed.

The larger purpose of the July ceremonies was to glorify the image of France at home and abroad by associating the current régime with the heroes of the Great Revolution and with the grandeur of the Napoleonic period. Indeed, for the observance of the return of Napoleon's ashes, which took place five months later, on 15 December 1840, Berlioz was yet again asked to write a triumphal march, something that almost compels one to say that he now had become the primary official composer of the régime. But Berlioz refused the new commission in order, as he confided to his sister Adèle, "to have the pleasure of seeing Auber, Halévy, and Adam fail miserably" in a genre to which he believed they were ill-suited and to which he had just contributed a work of major importance.

In fact those three composers did write funeral marches for the occasion, and, curiously enough, the one by Adam opens with a direct quotation from the opening of Berlioz's symphony – which movement Adam had earlier called an "inexplicable hotchpotch."[20] Was his gesture a parody? Or was it, as the solemnity of the circumstances would suggest, despite the "hotchpotch" remark, a tribute? Of the performance, Berlioz wrote that "It is simply impossible to imagine a fiasco more thorough and disgraceful than that experienced by those three poor devils." But Adam told a correspondent that while the works by Auber and Halévy produced little effect, his own had "had the pleasure of triumphing over those of his two illustrious rivals." Whom are we to believe? Even if Berlioz's report is accurate, the pleasure he took from the failure of his colleagues does not represent him at his magnanimous best. He behaved similarly, I am afraid, at the Parisian première of Wagner's *Tannhäuser*, in 1861, when the German composer's humiliation became in a sense the French composer's revenge.

In January 1842 (and again in September of that year), Berlioz revised the score of the *Symphonie funèbre* for concert performance, adding an optional part for strings to the original uncanny wind and brass sonorities, and a chorus heralding the glory of the heroes of July. Among those in the audience at the Salle Vivienne, when the new version was first given on 1 February 1842, was the (soon-to-be) composer of *Tannhäuser*: on the 5th, Richard Wagner told Robert Schumann that he found passages in the last movement of Berlioz's symphony so "magnificent and sublime that they can *never* be surpassed."

Love and music

In 1834, Nicolò Paganini had been disappointed that his request for a virtuoso concerto for solo viola had turned out to be a virtuoso symphony with obbligato viola. When he heard *Harold en Italie* for the first time, at Berlioz's concert of 16 December 1838, the Italian artist was so moved as to declare Berlioz the successor to Beethoven, and to offer him an extraordinarily generous "reward" of twenty thousand francs. With this handsome sum, Berlioz was able to pay his debts and to begin work on what became *Roméo et Juliette* – a new work, for contralto, tenor, and bass soloists, chorus, and orchestra, in the tradition of Beethoven's Ninth Symphony (as *Harold* had been), which became Berlioz's greatest encounter with the English poet who was the most hallowed figure in his sanctuary.

The *symphonie dramatique*, loosely adapted from Shakespeare into a seven-part symphony that is clearly the most avant-garde composition of the decade, was given in its entirety on three successive occasions in the autumn of 1839: the press was laudatory, the profits were meaningful, and Berlioz was inundated with compliments and congratulations from all quarters. The failure of *Cellini* could not be erased, the disappointment of lost royalties from multiple performances and arrangements could not be eradicated, but at the end of this fertile decade, even before the success of the *Symphonie funèbre* (which was seven months away), the composer's career was more than modestly afloat.

The high point of the dramatic symphony *Roméo et Juliette* – some think of Berlioz's œuvre as a whole – is not that operatic finale, in which a reconciliation of the embattled Montagues and Capulets is effected (and in which Friar Laurence sings an aria that elevates his importance well beyond that of the play), but rather the Adagio of the third movement, the deeply affective *Scène d'amour*. Here we have an expression of one of the central tenets of all of romantic music, for the rapture of the love between Romeo and Juliet is proclaimed not in the language of sung words, which would have been all too common-place, but rather in the language of purely instrumental music, which Berlioz recognized in preface to the published score as richer, of greater latitude, less restricted, and – by its very indistinctness, mysteriousness, ambiguity, and *vague* – incomparably more powerful than any other means of expression.

The opening page of the love scene, of all compositions properly called romantic, is among the few that merit the epithet sublime. Here violins, violas, and cellos activate a gently rocking texture in the com-pound meter that Berlioz often reserved for passionate expression; basses suggest a pulse, *pizzicato*, on a tonic pedal; English horn and clarinet whisper in unison, with brief phrases widely spaced, a frag-mentary melody. The atmosphere breathes with incipient desire; meanings are felt but not grasped. When Berlioz wrote, at the end of the *Mémoires*, that love "cannot give an idea of music," while music "can give an idea of love," he might well have pointed to this page, and said in his beloved Latin, *quod erat demonstrandum*.

The funeral march of the fifth movement, the *Convoi funèbre de Juliette*, provides another example of the "systematic" compositional behavior Berlioz regularly exhibited at moments of profound expres-sion. Here, in a note at the head of the score, the composer is out-spoken about his procedure: a fugal march is first played by the orchestra, with a single-note psalmody sung by the chorus; it is then *sung* by the chorus, with the psalmody taken over by the instruments. Accordingly we find a strict fugal texture woven beneath the Capulets' exhortation, in a measured rhythm that matches the inflection of the words, "Jetez des fleurs pour la vierge expirée" – "Strew flowers for the departed maiden." (When he wrote of the death of Harriet Smithson, Jules Janin cited this phrase.) At the mid-point of the movement the roles are reversed, the inflected rhythm is taken over by the strings in octaves, the mode shifts from the minor to the major, and the chorus sings the fugue. In fact the strictly imitative procedure of both halves is relaxed after the opening entries, as often occurs in Berlioz's fugues, but the impression that remains is that of unity within variety – the vocal and instrumental dwelling on the psalmodic note E, that is, in a myriad of harmonic contexts provided by the inevitably forward motion that is the hallmark of fugal texture. Here is a music that murmurs the geometry of its construction while it avoids the sound of mathematics; it shows its heart, as Schoenberg would say of the work of Brahms, while it shows its brain. This, in my view, is one of the most admirable and innovative aspects of Berlioz's compositional imagination.

When Berlioz wrote "normal" music, by which at the time most musicians meant music with "regular" phrases, his detractors cheered: "Berlioz has made great progress," said Adolphe Adam in 1840, after hearing the *Symphonie funèbre*, "because his phrases are now square-cut in units of four bars and are readily understandable."[21] Now, Adam was hardly an uneducated musician. But because he considered a melody a *malady* if it wasn't as square as a cube, he failed to see that Berlioz's use of varied phrase lengths resulted from the habit of avoiding filler, of keeping music in tune with a motivating dramatic idea. Indeed, the unexpected – l'*imprévu* – is, as Berlioz is at pains to say in the Postscript of the *Mémoires*, one of the chief characteristics of his music. Nowhere is this more obviously manifest than in the sixth movement of *Roméo et Juliette*, the tomb scene, *Roméo au tombeau des Capulets*. In a sequence that follows the acting version of

9 The opening page of the autograph of Part 6 of *Roméo et Juliette*, *Roméo au tombeau des Capulets*, with Berlioz's note suggesting that the typical concert public has no imagination.

the play by David Garrick that Berlioz knew and – despite its clear departure from Shakespeare's original – loved, we are urged to experience Romeo's tortured grief at the loss of Juliet and the terror he feels before her tomb. We are pressed to hear the ode he declaims to the *vierge expirée* (marked *Invocation*), to hear the couple's "delirious joy" on finding one another alive for one last, supreme moment (as they do in Garrick, not Shakespeare), and to hear their utter despair, final agony, and death.

In this wordless *scena* – as modern a music as Berlioz ever wrote – we detect fragments from earlier moments in the symphony (most obviously the love theme from the *Scène d'amour*) now transformed into whatever is the opposite of calm reflection, and we hear a new lamentation (the *Invocation*) whose ominous sonority (English horn, bassoon, and horn in unison) Verdi clearly remembered at the end of *Otello* (replacing the horn with the A clarinet) in order to sound the doom of another tragic pair of Shakespearean lovers. We hear a music whose logic requires imagination to perceive precisely because it is the logic of disjunction that closely follows the psychological progress of the action. This is what led Berlioz to affix the following note to the head of the score (see illustration 9):

> The public has absolutely no imagination; compositions which are addressed solely to the imagination therefore find absolutely no public. The following instrumental scene is in that category, and I believe that it ought always to be suppressed except when the symphony is performed before an élite group of listeners who are extremely familiar with the fifth act of Shakespeare's tragedy in the highly poetic version by Garrick. This is to say that it ought to be suppressed ninety-nine times out of a hundred. [...]

The note, sad in its recognition that a remarkable page was certain to be misunderstood, conveys a message that was eminently practical – for the page presented an extreme challenge to the orchestra and to any but the most experienced conductor. Others are advised to proceed from the *Convoi funèbre* directly to the operatic finale.

At the end of *Romeo and Juliet*, Shakespeare has Montague and Capulet vow to erect statues of the star-crossed lovers. This dramatic symphony is clearly Berlioz's "statue" to his own Juliet. But by 1840 or so, by which time her career had faded to nil, Harriet Smithson may have begun to feel that her husband, like the prototypical Frenchman, could not be trusted in love. Berlioz was no womanizer, but from his point of view, taking up with a mistress – often the privilege of the upper classes and hardly unusual in an age when sexual fidelity in marriage was but an option – may have been justified by an increasingly difficult domestic situation marked by an irksome jealousy that was long without foundation. After the first years of their marriage, Harriet began to take care neither of the house nor of herself; she had difficulty raising her son and supervising her servants; frequently ill, she kept the composer from sleeping and berated him in lengthy nocturnal tirades exacerbated by large doses of alcohol.

Was her ill humor provoked by that of her husband? His purpose for some years had been, after all, to win the hand of this Ophelia incarnate. When the prize he sought was won, the *raison d'être* of his tenacity was gone, and it was not long before what had been a heavenly goal became a burden very much of this earth. Consumed with earning a living as a composer, conductor, and journalist, Berlioz may have neglected his responsibilities at home; he never even found time to travel to La Côte to present his wife to his parents, and it was only when young Louis Berlioz was thirteen years old that he met his own grandfather. Whatever physical tenderness the couple enjoyed during the first years of their marriage obviously declined when Berlioz, against his wife's wishes, became a world traveler in the early eighteen-forties, and it evaporated after 1844, when he moved permanently out of their home.

It is not clear when Berlioz met Marie Martin, the woman who became his mistress and, later, his second wife. Her stage name, probably derived from a family name, was Récio, or Recio – both spellings are found in the records. It is possible that the original version of Berlioz's much prized song cycle, *Les Nuits d'été*, was conceived at the birth of his romance with Marie, and for her mezzo-soprano voice, in 1840. But three years earlier, at the first performance of the *Requiem*, on 5 December 1837, there was a Mlle Martin in the chorus. Could this have been Marie?²² She was born in 1814, outside Paris, of a French father who had been an officer in Napoleon's *Grande Armée*, and of a Spanish mother, Marie Sotera de Villas, who probably met Joseph Martin during Napoleon's Spanish campaign of 1808–14. None of Berlioz's previous biographers has known, as Marie presumably did, that her parents were not married. I was surprised to see Mme Sotera de Villas listed on Joseph Martin's corrected death certificate not as his *épouse*, but rather as his *gouvernante*. Growing up with the knowledge that her father's wife was living elsewhere, and with a daughter who would have been her half-sister, is surely something that helps to explain Marie's tenacity in her subsequent, sometimes tumultuous relationship with Berlioz.

Marie was a private voice student of the tenor Davidde Banderali, one of the Italian singers who had been invited to Paris by the Vicomte de La Rochefoucauld, in 1827, as a part of his scheme, engineered with Rossini's assistance, to revitalize the French school of singing via a transfusion of *ultramontane* blood. (Banderali, who in Italy had been the teacher of Giuditta Pasta, remained at the Paris Conservatoire until his death in 1849.) One may fairly suppose that it was her teacher who helped Marie to get a contract at the Opéra, where she was hired on 9 October 1841, and where she performed for one season in Rossini's *Comte Ory* (in the role of Isolier) and in Donizetti's *La Favorite* (in the role of Inès). Richard Wagner, who made a piano score of *La Favorite*, may well have seen Marie in that production. From all accounts she was a singer of very modest achievement: her technique was limited, her soprano register – according to a reviewer who heard her in Brussels in 1842 – somewhat shrill. The fact that Berlioz orchestrated the fourth song of *Les Nuits d'été* explicitly for Marie, however, militates against accepting such comments uncritically: *Absence*, simple in form and free of chromaticism, lies high for the singer – something that is hardly suited to a woman with a strident voice.

If it was probably in the interlude between the completion of *Roméo et Juliette* and the commission for the *Symphonie funèbre* that Berlioz began to call upon Marie, it was definitely at this time that he began drafting the songs for voice and piano that were published in the summer of 1841 as *Les Nuits d'été*. (The score carries a dedication to Louise Bertin, for whose compositional talents the composer seems to have had genuine respect.) Berlioz selected six poems from his friend Théophile Gautier's 1838 publication, *La Comédie de la mort*, that tell of lovers buoyant and sorrowful, near and far, alive and deceased, and he wove them into a non-narrative collection whose overarching quality is that of melancholy longing. Joseph d'Ortigue found an inspirational freshness in the simplicity of the original voice-and-piano settings, but most listeners have come to treasure songs in their incarnation as an orchestral cycle, which Berlioz completed sixteen years later, in 1856, at the invitation of the publisher Jakob Rieter-Biedermann. This Swiss businessman, after hearing the newly and ravishingly orchestrated *Le Spectre de la rose* in Gotha, on 6 February of that year, was so taken by it that he asked the composer to orchestrate the remaining Gautier songs, he purchased on the spot the rights to their publication, and he thus caused *Les Nuits d'été* to become the first orchestral cycle of its kind. Berlioz's dedications of the later versions to six different singers from the chapels in Weimar, Gotha, and Hanover suggest that they should be sung by women and men of various vocal ranges, and some current recordings follow this procedure. For the lone singer, performing all six *mélodies* without transposition can be a reach.

On the campaign trail

Berlioz's departure from Paris, for Brussels, on 20 September 1842, marked the beginning of a series of excursions abroad that eventually led to his stature as one of the most skilled itinerant composers of the century. He was already thirty-eight years old, but like Mozart, that youthful traveler par excellence, Berlioz, too, would gain from his *vagabondage* a cultural understanding and sophistication that marked his work, and that was unavailable by any other means.

It was an invitation from the prominent conductor François-Joseph Snell that prompted Berlioz to travel to Brussels. The two lengthy concerts he gave there, on 26 September and 9 October, were of mixed success, but he did enjoy an audience with King Leopold, and the satisfaction of the King's acceptance of the dedication of a specially prepared copy of the *Marche de pèlerins*, which was performed on both occasions. A projected concert in Frankfurt was aborted after Berlioz's arrival there in mid-October, and he returned home around the 20th of the month.

Less than two months later he undertook a far more ambitious concert tour that brought him back to the French capital only in May of the following year. This was an artistic "mission" – the first of many – primarily to make known the newly expressive instrumental music that he had written and that he took to be the logical consequence of Beethoven's symphonic achievement. But it was also an *official* mission, sponsored by the administration, to gather information regarding German musical institutions, and to learn what was to be feared or to be hoped from their progress. Accordingly, over the next five months, Berlioz established relationships with eminent foreign musicians, rekindled old friendships, learned the rigors of international travel, and perfected the art of the globe-trotting conductor. He also became highly knowledgeable about musical conditions in Germany and reported on them not only in a series of articles for the *Journal des débats*, which we have long known, but also, in condensed form, to the Minister of the Interior.

Indeed, that Minister, the Comte Duchatel, had authorized Berlioz's paid absence from his post in the library at the Conservatoire precisely because he had charged the composer with "gathering information useful to the administration."[23] The report that Berlioz eventually submitted, on 28 December 1843, concluded with a résumé of his findings in Germany: he had discovered a nearly total absence of highly gifted singers capable of dramatic performance, and theater choruses of decided mediocrity, but fine singing schools and magnificent military bands; few worthwhile new compositions, but many excellent orchestras (though "*none* in any way comparable to the orchestra of the Conservatoire in Paris"); widespread musical knowledge among the general populace; generous pension funds not only for musicians employed by the theaters but also for independent composers; and a constructive influence exerted upon the arts by church and state alike.

Berlioz expressed regret to the Minister for not having had time to report on German conservatories, which suggests that such an investigation, along with the possible recruitment of singers, was also a part of his charge. Thus, what has usually been seen as a mission undertaken by Berlioz to establish his reputation abroad and thus strengthen his position at home, and to challenge the mediocrity of so much contemporary music by performing selections of his own, must also be seen as a mission of the literal sort, underwritten by the government and deemed by one of its chief ministers to have been highly constructive indeed. As the Comte Duchatel later wrote to Berlioz, on 14 February 1844, after reading his report: "I thank you for the enlightened determination and enthusiasm that you have brought to your task, and I am pleased to have been able to offer you a way of employing your profound knowledge of music in such a useful manner."

For every concert that Berlioz gave abroad, there is a tale of trial and tribulation joined to a tale of appreciation and, occasionally, adulation. In Leipzig, he renewed his friendship with Mendelssohn, whom he had known in Rome in 1831, and he spent a good deal of time with Robert Schumann, whose diary tells us of his appreciation of the Frenchman's resourcefulness and originality. At Berlioz's concert of 4 February 1843, Schumann heard the Overtures to *Les Francs-Juges* and *Le Roi Lear*, the *Symphonie fantastique*, the *Rêverie et Caprice* for violin and orchestra (written in 1841 on the basis of an aria removed from the score of *Benvenuto Cellini*), and two songs, *La Belle Voyageuse* (from the *Neuf Mélodies* of 1829, newly revised for mezzo-soprano and orchestra) and *Absence* (not yet orchestrated), sung by Marie Récio. He also heard the *Offertoire* of the *Requiem* (which Berlioz gave separately on many occasions during his career): in this movement, superimposed upon a highly complex polyphonic texture, the chorus is reduced to two notes, A and B flat, which occur in a variety of harmonic contexts until, at the end, the many-times-repeated B flat becomes a B natural, the music is transmuted from a dark D minor to a radiant D major, and the offering is transformed into a veritable hymn of love. For Schumann, the *Offertoire* – one of Berlioz's "systematic" works that never gives the impression of constraint (the *Dignare* of the later *Te Deum* is another) – surpassed "everything."

In Dresden, where Berlioz gave two concerts in mid-February, he saw Wagner, whom he had met in Paris in 1839, and whose assistance with rehearsals now he much appreciated. (When he returned to Dresden eleven years later, in 1854, Berlioz was offered the same position that Wagner now occupied, that of second Kapellmeister to the King of Saxony, the first position still nominally occupied by the composer Karl Reissiger.) Berlioz gave further concerts in Hechingen, Mannheim, Weimar, Brunswick, Hamburg, Berlin, Hanover, and Darmstadt, offering varied programs with excerpts from the symphonies, from the *Requiem*, and from *Benvenuto Cellini*, and further vocal selections in which the most frequent soloist was Marie Récio.

My assumption is that when he first met Marie, Berlioz was frankly taken by her apparent sexuality. Berlioz called Marie "les yeux noirs" – sounding rather like one of George Sand's lovestruck companions – and it was surely not for nothing that the young Eduard Hanslick spoke of Marie, in 1846, as Berlioz's "fiery-eyed Spanish lady." Berlioz was also taken by Marie's strength, I should think, later referring to her, with mixed emotions, as his "*homme d'affaires.*" I have said that we know nothing of the explicit sparks that lit the blaze between them, but we do know that the fires began to cool, at least momentarily, during this very tour in Germany. Together with her in Weimar in

January 1843, Berlioz then left the city without Marie, apparently troubled by her insistence on appearing at all of his concerts and possibly disappointed with the results. That she sang "like a cat" – Ferdinand Hiller's recollection of Berlioz's comment at the time – is not fully believable, however, given Berlioz's standards, though this sort of locker-room talk may indeed have occurred between friends who had shared the favors of another highly erotic woman more than a decade earlier. Berlioz's "flight" (which lasted for only a day or two) may have been provoked as much by the tension of traveling with a mistress (which can be particularly awkward when one has a famous wife, alive if not well, back in Paris) as by any antipathy for Marie, musical or other.

After Berlioz's concert tour of 1842–43, Marie Récio appeared on the stage on only rare occasion. In the autumn of 1843 she briefly took the role of Charlotte in a revival of Auber's *L'Ambassadrice*, at the Opéra Comique. For the *Concert spirituel* of Palm Sunday, on 6 April 1844, Berlioz added a counterpoint for Marie's solo soprano to the solo tenor part in the *Sanctus* of the *Requiem*. That this part is now never performed is unfortunate, I think, for it is lovely, if simple, and may have sounded well in Marie's rendition. In June of that year she was soloist in a cantata by Michele-Enrico Carafa given at a concert to raise money for the reconstruction of the ancient Carmelite monastery in what is now northwestern Israel. Marie then seems largely to have joined her energies to those of her now permanent companion. Berlioz began openly to use her address in 1844 – she lived only three blocks away from his official apartment – by which time the relationship with Harriet had reached the point of no return.

In January 1843, while Berlioz was on the road, the prominent art patron Baron Taylor, along with the composers Meyerbeer, Auber, and Halévy, the pianists Thalberg and Liszt, and the publisher Maurice Schlesinger, organized a cooperative Association des artistes musiciens, of which Berlioz was invited to become one of five executive secretaries. The purpose of this union, given the increasing isolation of the musician in a social fabric that tended to value more obviously "productive" individuals, and a government more attuned to commissioning works from painters, sculptors, and architects than to caring for the needs of performing musicians, was to create an endowment that would support pensions and other financial benefits for those whose livelihood came essentially from playing in the pit. The endowment would be augmented by regular contributions from the members (of whom there were over six thousand by 1854), by special lotteries, and by occasional concerts – which, of course, were to be Berlioz's particular domain. He would become honorary vice-president of the Association in 1857, but his principal activities for the group took place essentially during the first decade of its existence. In the fall of 1843, he planned a special fund-raising "festival" concert, but the various fees demanded by the directors of the Théâtre Italien and the Opéra for the use of their premises, and Berlioz's own rivalry with Habeneck (the conductor of the orchestras at the Opéra and at the Conservatoire, who always felt that the right of first refusal was his), led to the abandonment of the idea.[24]

In the summer of 1844 Berlioz took up his scepter as the "official" composer of the July Monarchy with his *Hymne à la France*, a setting of a text by Auguste Barbier with an oft-repeated refrain of "God protect France." And with this work he achieved a patriotic triumph – for the work was performed by more than a thousand musicians at a festival concert in the great hall of the Exhibition of French Industry then on display, and it was received enthusiastically by an audience of more than eight times that number. Berlioz gave another festival concert (by which he usually meant the execution of music on a grand scale by a group of composers) in the spring of 1845, at the Cirque Olympique, an imposing structure along the Champs-Elysées completed one year earlier as an equestrian circus palace. He would later direct mammoth performances in 1855, at the Palais de l'Industrie, and in 1867, at the time of the largest Universal Exhibition the world had ever seen.

Caricatures of Berlioz conducting in the midst of masses of motley musicians testify to his reputation as the first real master of concerts appropriately labeled "monster."

In October 1845, Berlioz undertook his second major European tour – another five-month jaunt that led him to Vienna, Prague, Pest, Breslau, and Brunswick before returning him to Paris at the beginning of May 1846. In Vienna, where he stayed from November 1845 to January 1846, he was introduced to the aged Metternich (who years earlier had thought Berlioz some sort of *agent provocateur*), and he stood for a portrait by August Prinzhofer that he found especially true to life (see illustration 10). In Prague, in January 1846, he met the musical scholar August Wilhelm Ambrose, who mistook Marie Récio for Harriet Smithson, and was informed by a morbidly humorous Berlioz that his "first wife" was "dead" – when in fact she was back in Paris, distraught, but still very much alive. And he met the soon-to-be-celebrated critic Eduard Hanslick, who wrote an enthusiastic and perceptive review of the three concerts that Berlioz gave in that musically minded city, which had so warmly welcomed Mozart some fifty years before:

> I beseech you, study Berlioz's scores, and you will see that there is in them, along with all the spontaneity, an admirable intellectual coherence; and, along with all the passion, a solid, orderly design at the core. Study his scores and you will grasp and admire the powerful conceptions of the Master; and, when the large-scale contours of the whole become clear to you, you will easily discover the coherence of the smallest periods.[25]

"Ritter Berlioz in Prague," the title of Hanslick's essay, might have been transformed into "Chevalier Berlioz" in Breslau, or Brunswick, or Pest – Berlioz merited the honorary title as from 1839, when he was awarded the distinction of Chevalier de la Légion d'honneur – for on this occasion he was well received almost everywhere he went.

At the beginning of June 1846 (he had been home for about a month), Berlioz was asked by his friend Jules Janin and by the

10 August Prinzhofer's lithograph of the composer, made in Vienna in 1845.
Berlioz denied ever wearing rings and carrying a cane, but none the less
suggested, in 1850, that this portrait was the one that resembled him the most.

Municipal Council of Lille to write the music for a cantata to celebrate the opening of the new rail line that linked Paris to that growing northern city – the achievement of the Baron James de Rothschild's Compagnie du Chemin de fer du Nord and an improvement in the means of national and international travel which Berlioz would much value. Reluctantly interrupting more important work, the composer consoled himself with the thought, humorously noted later, that the fatherland did have "the right to ask from each of its children an unquestioning devotion." He reminded himself that he, too, was a "child of the fatherland" (paraphrasing the opening line of the *Marseillaise*, "Allons, enfants de la patrie"), and spent a week setting Janin's occasional poem to music. The *Chant des chemins de fer*, for solo tenor, chorus, and orchestra, with its five-times repeated refrain celebrating the "soldiers of peace" who built the railroad, was first performed in the splendiferous presence of the king's sons Montpensier and Nemours, four ministers, Hugo, Lamartine, Ingres, and seventeen hundred invited guests. It is one of those works, like *Le Cinq Mai* (written in 1835 to commemorate the death of Napoleon Bonaparte), which lead critics to call Berlioz's œuvre uneven. Just or not, such criticism ought not to fail to acknowledge the desire the composer clearly felt to participate in the creation of some sort of "public art": the railroad cantata and others of Berlioz's overtly political works are descendants of the festival hymns of the Revolution of 1789, and evidence of his sporadic efforts to provide *nobles jouissances* or elevated enjoyment for the general French population.

The "more important" work that had had momentarily to be set aside was *La Damnation de Faust*, which the composer had set down in fits and starts during his recent travels in Austria, Hungary, Bohemia, and Silesia. Taking up his first musical reaction to Goethe's masterpiece, the *Huit Scènes de Faust* of 1829, Berlioz enlarged that brief collection of separate numbers into a radical sort of concert opera of over two hours' duration, which he chose definitively to label a *légende dramatique*. Unlike Gounod, who later made a pretty love story of Goethe's complex text (and in so doing created the most popular of all nineteenth-century French operas), Berlioz created a mixed-genre successor to *Roméo et Juliette* whose scenic power is best seen in the eye of the mind. He portrays Goethe's principal figures in concentrated segments, without operatic filler, and against a background of an all-encompassing Nature. Berlioz's Faust is not so much the eternally striving figure of the German drama, but rather a personage – isolated, restless, and devastated by alienation from society and *ennui* – with whom the French composer could more readily identify.

This is a score of incomparable richness and variety, a carefully ordered aggregation of relatively short and intense musical numbers, a grand and idiosyncratic amalgamation of styles learned, popular, fantastical, lyrical, and dramatic. But despite the overall receptivity of the critics in the aftermath of the first performances, which Berlioz gave at the Opéra Comique on 6 and 20 December 1846, the financial losses he experienced on those occasions were catastrophic. Even more deeply wounding, as Berlioz recalled in chapter 54 of the *Mémoires*, was the unexpected indifference of the public, which led him to vow never again to stake even twenty francs on the approval of his music by an audience in Paris. It is ironic that in France, in the twentieth century, partly because the work was (dubiously but popularly) staged by Raoul Gunsbourg in 1893, partly because it was the favorite of Berlioz's first exhaustive biographer, Adolphe Boschot,[26] *La Damnation de Faust* became the composer's best-liked work.

Berlioz undertook a third international concert tour in February 1847, traveling this time via Brussels and Berlin to Saint-Petersburg, Moscow, Riga (then incorporated into Russia), and, via Berlin, back to Paris, where he arrived four months later, at the beginning of July. In Saint-Petersburg he gave the first two parts of the *Damnation* (the Faust sang in French, the Mephistopheles, in German) – and he had a brief amatory adventure with a seamstress who sang in the chorus. From his subsequent exchange of letters with the French cellist Dominique Tajan-Rogé (who played in the Imperial Orchestra there), we can glean a few details of this encounter. In retrospect Berlioz seems to have been embarrassed by having had a liaison with a young woman of no social distinction (although she did speak five languages), and yet he was so smitten as to have considered taking her off with him and abandoning everything else. The lady was apparently engaged to be married, however, and thus declined to respond to Berlioz's further advances, which continued until at least the end of 1847. Tajan-Rogé, a convinced Saint-Simonian, chastised Berlioz for what we might call his "class bias," saying that had Berlioz taken a mistress of high station, such as the Comtesse Marie d'Agoult, he would have rather made of it a public announcement. Someone ought to pursue this intriguing, and potentially revealing, suggestion.

In Berlin, on 19 June, Berlioz gave a complete performance of *La Damnation de Faust* that was apparently met by opposition from some who thought a Frenchman had no right to tamper with Goethe's revered masterpiece. Charges of having "mutilated" Goethe's magnum opus echoed well into the twentieth century, sometimes based on opposition to Berlioz's transmogrification of the text (he had written much of it himself, with the assistance of the little-known journalist Almire Gandonnière), sometimes based on opposition to the very notion of setting to music (and thus disabling) the now canonized verbal drama.

Berlioz recovered from these musical and emotional vicissitudes – as well as those provoked by his hopeful but eventually futile discussions with the administration regarding his appointment as conductor at the Opéra – during his next major excursion, this one to London, where he assumed the post of music director at the Drury Lane Theater in November 1847, having signed a contract to work there with the impresario Louis-Antoine Jullien. After making a fine beginning with well-received performances of operas by Donizetti and Balfe, Berlioz soon came to realize, while rehearsing every afternoon at 4 and conducting every evening at 7, that his employer's enterprise was built on a highly fragile financial base. Yet even in the absence of a regular paycheck from the little-experienced and apparently half-crazed Jullien, he felt secure enough in London, as a kind of successor to the much admired Felix Mendelssohn (who had died on 4 November 1847, the very day of Berlioz's arrival in the English capital) to "erase France" from his musical topography. Like Beethoven in Vienna, Berlioz in London was prepared to free himself from the circumstances of his past and to flourish in the conditions of exile.

Soon, however, despite the warm reception his music received from the English public, and the warm reception he himself received in social and musical circles, he began to think of further concert tours in Germany and Russia. And he began to feel what all Frenchmen feel after long absence from the fatherland, the lack of friends and family and of the familiar exasperations of home. After an artistically rich but financially unrewarding concert in the Hanover Square Rooms, where he gave excerpts from *Harold en Italie* and the *Damnation de Faust*, Berlioz published a gracious letter of thanks and farewell to the English musicians and amateurs he had come to respect and admire, and, on 11 July 1848, he sailed for France.

Marie, who probably knew about Berlioz's little Russian romance and subsequent choral lament, had joined him in England in April; she remained by his side – stubbornly? faithfully? – for the rest of her life. To his old friend from Roman days, Joseph-Louis Duc, Berlioz recounted seeing a brilliant *Hamlet* in London in 1848, noting that "Marie and I left the theater literally exhausted, trembling, and intoxicated with grief and admiration." It is pleasant to know that the composer was able to share with his traveling companion his lifelong passion for Shakespeare, something that speaks well for Marie's education at a time when, in certain circles, the literate woman was still considered "dangerous." "I am leaving the day after tomorrow for the living hell that is Paris," Berlioz told his sister on 11 July 1848. "I don't yet know where I shall reside." Harriet was living alone in Montmartre, and Berlioz was supporting her from afar. He obviously planned to live with his mistress; he could certainly not rejoin his wife.

The "grief and admiration" Berlioz felt after seeing *Hamlet*, in May, found expression sixth months later, in November, when he revised the *Marche funèbre* he had conceived in 1844 for the last scene of the play. If ever there was a musical symbol of Berlioz's despair over the "nothingness" of it all – a despair incited by the revolution on the continent in February and exacerbated by the death of his father in July – it is here, in this brief but tragic monument, whose key, rhythmic ostinato, and tempo marking are taken over from the second movement of Beethoven's Seventh Symphony (one of the selections performed at Berlioz's funeral). In the Beethoven the relentlessness of the A minor opening is relieved by a contrasting section in the parallel major; in the Berlioz, contrast with the lugubrious principal melody comes in the form of an oft-repeated two-bar flourish that would symbolize, should one wish to read the work in this way, the grand royal figure that Hamlet, in Fortinbras's words, would have proven to be. The Beethoven also suggested to Berlioz a way of concluding without absolute closure: the Allegretto of the Seventh Symphony ends as it begins, with a second-inversion, "unstable" harmony; the *Hamlet* March ends not with the root of the tonic triad but with the third, sustained by the chorus for a few beats beyond the final chord. Listen to this nine-minute threnody, marvel at its inventive maneuvers, and wonder why it is so little known.

3   Introspection (1848–1869)

Republican agitation and imperial redress

When Berlioz arrived in Paris in 1821, the city – already the largest on the continent – had a population of approximately three-quarters of a million. By the time of the February Revolution of 1848, the population was over one million, and by 1870 it was well over two. As the industrial revolution altered patterns of employment in the capital, gradually larger numbers began to use leisure time for exposure to literature and the arts, and Paris became "the undisputed dynamo," in Nigel Gosling's words, "from which western culture drew its power."[1] This is certainly the image of the capital, and of the country, that is projected in the painting by Janet-Lange reproduced on the following page of this chapter (see illustration 11).

It could therefore come as a surprise to hear Berlioz assert, in a letter of 26 May 1848, that "You have to have a tri-colored flag over your eyes in order not to see that music in France is now dead." The turmoil of the time explains the exaggeration of the term. In fact, while his disillusionment with the events of 1848 was shared by many intellectuals, Berlioz met the news as he had in 1830, this time preparing (while still in England) a new version of *La Marseillaise*, arrangements of Méhul's once popular *Chant du départ* and Rouget de Lisle's *Mourons pour la patrie* (now lost), and a draft of *La Menace des Francs*, whose text celebrates the toppling by the people of an unpopular king. Berlioz's English publisher also brought out a new arrangement for chorus and piano of the

11 *La France éclairant le monde*, Janet-Lange's expression of the country's
progressive aspirations at the time of the Revolution of 1848. (A lithograph
portrait of Berlioz by Janet-Lange appeared in *L'Illustration* on 18 May 1844.)

Apothéose from the *Symphonie funèbre et triomphale*, which the composer
thought would be timely and thus a good sell in Paris. For the occasion,
to the earlier verses that had been provided by Antony Deschamps,
Berlioz added several couplets of his own, further glorifying the heroes
of the July Revolution and celebrating the notion of "liberté," once
again at issue in revolutionary times, as the "honneur de la patrie."

These activities seem in contrast with what most occupied Berlioz in 1847 and 1848, the compiling of his *Mémoires* – whose preface is dated "London, 21 March 1848," less than one month after Louis-Philippe's abdication – for much of that book, too, seems designed to show that "the art of music, for so long in a state of decay, is now quite dead." In the last months of that fateful year, now back in Paris, Berlioz completed and polished the greater part of the volume which, more vividly than any other, has conveyed to generations the story of his life.

Books called *Mémoires* are problematical: they suggest veracity, but shun the appearance of testimony before a tribunal, and thus, when well written, become art – that is, fiction. Perhaps Berlioz should have called his book *Histoire de mes idées*, as did the contemporary historian Edgar Quinet, or, if not *Confessions*, following Rousseau, perhaps *Professions of Faith*. These titles avoid the ambiguity of *Mémoires*, but they, too, cannot be properly read unless one is alert to those passages that disguise reality in order to promote coherence. It is true that the more we learn about Berlioz from his letters and other contemporary documents, the more we see the essential truths upon which the *Mémoires* are built. It is also true that when the *Mémoires* are in conflict with contemporary documents, the latter are likely to be more accurate, if less poetic, than the book.

Writing *Mémoires* was a common enough activity in the French nineteenth century, so much so that even Louis-Philippe contributed to the genre with a volume that suggests a sharp intelligence and a watchful temperament. If such literary activity was limited among musicians (Grétry is Berlioz's best-known predecessor; Gounod, a notable successor), it is because few had the literary bent of our composer. His earliest gods were Virgil, Shakespeare, and Goethe; Chateaubriand, too, was a favorite, and Berlioz's appetite for setting down a narrative of his life, in 1848, was surely stimulated by the author of the *Génie du christianisme*, who had arranged for his own *Mémoires d'outre-tombe* to appear immediately after his death (which occurred on 4 July 1848). It is not inconceivable that Berlioz's friend Armand Bertin, editor of the *Journal des débats* and earlier

Chateaubriand's private secretary, encouraged the dominant figure of French romantic music (as Berlioz had a right to think of himself) to prepare memoirs along the lines of those of the dominant figure of French romantic literature.

But acting more powerfully on his imagination than the literary enticement was the political reality of the revolution in France, which Berlioz liked to call "the end of the world." Arrived at this point, what more logical than to self-interrogate, to introspect – to reflect upon one's existence, to justify one's actions, to lament one's fate and laugh at one's foibles, and to express (and thereby perhaps to assuage) one's despair. On 15 March 1848 Berlioz wrote from London to Joseph d'Ortigue that not only were the arts in France now dead, but that music, too, was beginning to decompose: "let it be buried soon," he quipped, "for I can smell its noxious vapors from here." We may smile at such bitter imagery, not because we doubt its sincerity – for others at the time deplored the effect on the arts of such revolutionary turmoil – but because we appreciate its style. It is by its style that Berlioz's book is distinguished from so many others (including Chateaubriand's), and it is by its wit that the book lives on today.

The letter of thanks that Berlioz published in the Morning Post when he left England, in July, had opened on a note of resignation: "I am going away, back to the country which is still called France ['even though a new Republic had been proclaimed on 26 February' is the implication], and which after all is my own." If his departure was motivated by sentimental allegiance to his nation, it was also motivated by the uncertainty of his prospects in England, where the numbers of his adversaries were gaining on the numbers of his friends. In France, of course, his enemies had always been as noisy as his admirers. But when he arrived in Paris, he was able to rescue his position as librarian at the Conservatoire, thanks to the intervention of Victor Hugo (who had been elected to the legislature as a deputy from Paris) and to resume his writing for the Journal des débats and the Revue et Gazette musicale.

Meanwhile, in July, stirred by the winds of change, the Association des artistes musiciens was attempting to improve the lot of the musician with the establishment of a new concert hall, with additional offices and facilities for the printing of music. Berlioz, along with Halévy, Auber, Spontini, Habeneck, and others signed a petition to this effect that was addressed to the new Minister of the Interior, but nothing seems to have come of their effort.[2] The National Assembly did vote, on the 17th, to accord two hundred thousand francs to the artistic community in order to relieve those who had been displaced during the uprising of February and the disorder of the following several months, but Berlioz, who plaintively observed the pianists playing on the sidewalks and the painters sweeping the streets, felt certain that such an outlay was insufficient to make any real difference.

Berlioz's father died in time of revolution, on the fateful anniversary of 28 July 1848. The composer had for so long tried to win the old man's approval that he became momentarily disoriented when the principal object of his travail was no more. Delacroix's *Liberty Leading the People*, titled *le 28 juillet*, would now be, for Berlioz, a mixed metaphor indeed. He traveled to La Côte in August and spent several weeks at home, there to share the loss with his family. Psychoanalytic biographers have long capitalized upon Wolfgang Mozart's relationship with Leopold; Berlioz's relationship with his own father would surely prove to be an equally valuable investment.

A little more than one month after returning to Paris, on 29 October 1848, Berlioz directed a *grande fête musicale*, for the benefit of the Association des artistes musiciens, in the royal opera house at Versailles: in addition to his own music – *La Captive* (the seductive *mélodie* he had composed in Italy in 1832, now in its sixth and definitive arrangement for contralto and orchestra), *L'Invitation à la valse* (the piece for piano, by Weber, that Berlioz had orchestrated in 1841), and excerpts from *Roméo* and *Faust* – Berlioz conducted music by Beethoven, Rossini, Mozart, and Gluck. "My compositions in particular were tremendously successful," he wrote after the concert, but he was chagrined that the substantial profits went not to him, but to the treasury of the Association. To his sister he could not resist adding a cynical note about the politics of the event:

> At the concert there was a party from the *Government* among whom was M. Marrast [the president of the National Assembly], who had *insisted* on sitting in the royal chair. Consequently, the noble place in the middle of the upper gallery has now been occupied by five sovereigns: Louis XV, Louis XVI, Louis-Philippe I, Napoleon I, and Marrast. O!!!!

In public Berlioz presumably reined in his more skeptical thoughts about the leaders of the new Republic, something that may have helped when he received five hundred francs from the Minister of the Interior (on 7 February 1849) simply in his capacity as "compositeur de musique." But in private, even Lamartine (whose verse he admired) did not escape his barbs: when Cuvillier-Fleury published a scathing review of Lamartine's *Histoire de la Révolution de 1848* in the still very much Orleanist *Journal des débats* of 16 August 1849, Berlioz told his sister that "it is impossible to find anything better written, more sensible, and more cruel" than his journalistic colleague's "devastating flagellation" of the "vainglorious" poet who had been a leading voice in the establishment of the new régime. Democratic republic, Berlioz felt, was not conducive to art.

It was therefore to his liking, as the smoke of the latest revolution began to clear, that the legislative assembly approved a new constitution with a strong executive authority, for this cleared the way for the ascension of Louis Napoleon Bonaparte. Relying primarily on the fact that he was his famous uncle's nephew, the embodiment of a legend and (rightly or wrongly) the symbol of order and prosperity, this Napoleon rose to the top of the heap of candidates for the presidency, won an overwhelming victory, and, on 20 December 1848, found himself triumphantly inaugurated as President for a four-year term.

Berlioz had met Louis Napoleon in London, less than a year earlier, in February 1848, when, on the basis of letters of introduction provided by Alfred de Vigny, he was invited to a soirée given by Lady

Blessington, the Comte Alfred d'Orsay's mistress, at Gore House, in Kensington. (The Imperial Pretender to the throne, imprisoned after two abortive attempts to seize power, in 1836 and 1840, had escaped to London in the autumn of 1846, and was there living the fashionably good life while preparing for the demise of Louis-Philippe.) The composer seems to have formed a positive impression of the would-be ruler, though he made sport of Louis' public speaking, which, far from polished oratory, was limited by his thin voice and German accent, the result of having been brought up abroad. Shortly after "the man of destiny" returned to France and became President of the Republic, Berlioz chanced upon him in public on several occasions. "Yesterday, on the boulevard, I happened to meet the President," he told his sister on 20 July 1849; "we recognized and greeted each other in the most friendly possible way." Berlioz joked about giving the President the impression that he could always count on the musician's electoral vote, even though Berlioz was no advocate of universal suffrage. For him, this period of *liberté*, *fraternité*, and *égalité* was one of misery, immorality, and stupidity, in which few seemed to care a whit about the arts.

It was therefore with pleasure that he greeted Louis Napoleon's seizure of absolute authority on 2 December 1851. As he wrote on the 9th, "this *coup d'état* is the work of a master; indeed, it is a veritable masterpiece." He went in person to present his compliments to the newly fortified President and sang his praises to friends and family alike. Again, when the people voted to make Napoleon their Emperor, in November 1852, Berlioz was delighted. One might want to suggest that his delight was based on self-interest, for he did have reason to believe that his *Te Deum* would be performed at an Imperial Coronation in the Cathedral of Notre Dame. (Berlioz had drafted the *Te Deum* in 1848 and 1849; he thought of the colossal *Judex crederis* at the end as a "brother," or "cousin," to the *Requiem*, although the work is otherwise of relatively intimate sonority.) No such ceremony took place, however, nor was the *Te Deum* performed at the Imperial Marriage on 30 January 1853, despite the composer's effort to remind the Emperor of his existence on the 7th by presenting him with a copy of his newly published book, Les Soirées de l'orchestre, and with a plan for the organization of a new Imperial Chapel (of which not he, but Auber, became director).

Such disappointments did not discourage Berlioz from remaining a Bonapartiste. He explicitly told his sister that his admiration for the Emperor was "disinterested," that this Napoleon was "magnificently reasonable, logical, strong, and decisive," even if he would have little time to consider matters of art and would be surrounded by the usual old men with the usual old ideas. During the early years of the Second Empire and well into the eighteen-sixties, Berlioz remained grateful to Napoleon III for "delivering" France from "that filthy and stupid republic" – a sentiment he took to be shared by "all civilized men." In 1856, when his sister Adèle chided him for insufficiently praising the Sovereign (in his newspaper account of the vacation towns of "Plombières et Bade," of 4 September), Berlioz pleaded not guilty: the editor of the Journal des débats had in fact angered Berlioz by removing an entire section devoted to the Emperor – so much so that Berlioz considered taking his column to the rival Constitutionnel. He was persuaded not to do so by Armand Bertin, who explained that "the Journal des débats," which relied upon the support of the old Orléanistes, "cannot praise the Emperor." Later, when the Princess Wittgenstein praised the Emperor and doubted Berlioz's allegiance to him, he replied, on 30 August 1864, that on the contrary she was preaching to the converted: "I am and have always been one of the Emperor's admirers, and I do not see why you appear to doubt this fact. He himself is well aware of it."

Towards the end of 1849, while Louis Napoleon undertook to strengthen his prestige as President, Berlioz undertook to establish a Grande Société Philharmonique de Paris. This was not the first time he participated in such a venture, for even as a student at the Conservatoire, in 1828, with his friend Stephen de la Madelaine (a chapel singer at the court of Charles X), he had attempted to found a similarly independent organization. This was a Société du Gymnase-

Lyrique, projected in the aftermath of the successful opening season of the Société des Concerts du Conservatoire, with sixty-five instrumentalists and fifty-five singers, designed to provide young French composers with the opportunity "to become known to the public via concerts equal in brilliance to the best the capital has to offer."[3] Berlioz's function was that of the Premier Commissaire, who was to recruit the musicians, prepare the scores and parts, and coach the singers (something that tells us that his vocal talents were both genuine and appreciated by his associates).

That Société du Gymnase-Lyrique failed to take root, for Cherubini took it as unwelcome competition for the Société des Concerts du Conservatoire and persuaded the Vicomte de La Rochefoucauld to deny its request for governmental assistance. Now, in 1849, Berlioz sought out the President of the Republic himself, on 5 December, in order to gain support for his new Société Philharmonique. A meeting with Louis Napoleon could not be arranged at that time, but Berlioz would have said to him what he wrote in the prospectus of the organization: "The City of Paris used to lack one of those grand musical societies that grace the principal capitals of Europe: London, Vienna, Brussels, Saint Petersburg. Such an important institution has just been founded."[4] This was a cooperative enterprise (like the Société des Concerts) that would feature some of the finest singers of the capital, some new music by lesser-known composers, some familiar items by Berlioz's heroes, and a sprinkling of music of his own. The concerts would be given in the Salle Sainte-Cécile, off the Chausée d'Antin, in an auditorium that proved to be not fully satisfactory. At the end of the first season, in May 1850, Berlioz therefore made an effort to obtain the use of the better suited concert hall of the Conservatoire, writing to the Minister of the Interior as follows:

> Monsieur le Ministre
> The Grande Société Philharmonique de Paris, inaugurated last February in the Salle Sainte-Cécile, has rendered service to the art of music such that we now dare to hope that you will deem it worthy of your esteemed protection. Comprised of two hundred artists to whom it has provided unhoped for opportunities for performance,

the Society puts its full resources at the disposal of young composers who have returned from Rome and who, while holders of government stipends, find no possibility of performance offered to them by any other Parisian musical institution.[5]

This letter is signed by the members of the group's executive committee: the cellist Prosper Seligmann, the violinist Jean-Marie Becquié, the cellist Dominique Tajan-Rogé, the pianist and critic Léon Kreutzer, the violinist Lambert Massart, the composer Auguste Morel, and by Berlioz, who asks that the Minister reply to his address at 19, rue de Boursault, where he was then living with Marie Récio. On 25 May the Minister replied courteously that the hall at the Conservatoire was available only to the Société des Concerts. Berlioz's musicians – like the artists of a later decade who organized a *Salon des refusés* – would have to organize their own show.

The minutes of Berlioz's organization indicate that on the question of repertory there was some dissension in the ranks, but the failure to obtain the one decent concert hall in Paris was a far more ominous sign that the orchestra would be short lived. The seventh and last concert of the 1850–51 season took place on 29 April 1851, after which the Société Philharmonique de Paris ceased to exist. Things might have turned out differently had the Minister been sufficiently concerned to impose his will upon that of the director of the Conservatoire, as the Vicomte de La Rochefoucauld had once done for Berlioz twenty-two years earlier, but the current Interior Minister, Pierre-Jules Baroche, had been appointed only two months before, and while occupied with matters directly pertaining to the society of the fledgling Second Republic, he had no time for the Société Philharmonique.

Meanwhile, by a government decree dated 27 April 1850, Berlioz did become Bibliothécaire du Conservatoire – head librarian – after the death of his longtime superior, and friend, Bottée de Toulmon. The post that he had occupied, of *adjoint*, was discontinued, but most of the work continued to be done, as in the past, by another longtime assistant, César Leroy, whose career at the library extended from 1830 – four years before a new copyright law led to the library's receipt of all new publications in music (and thus to a great deal of cataloguing) – until his death in 1871. Berlioz's initial salary at the library, in 1839, had been fifteen hundred francs per year. On 1 January 1852, fifteen months after he assumed the title of librarian-in-chief, it was increased to twenty-five hundred francs. One year later, on 1 January 1853, for reasons unknown, it was reduced to the original amount.[6]

If the administration of Louis Napoleon offered no support to the Société Philharmonique, Louis' Minister of Commerce did take an interest in Berlioz when he asked him, in April 1851, to serve on a commission to judge the merits of musical instruments at the Great Exhibition of Works of Industry of All Nations held at the wondrous Crystal Palace, in London. ("Industry" did not include "Art," of course, but the *making* of instruments was indeed a *métier*.) That the best qualified person was actually enlisted for jury duty suggests that this Minister actually knew what he was doing: Louis-Joseph Buffet hailed from Mirecourt, the provincial capital of violin-making at the time, where half the town's population was engaged in that occupation, and a smaller number in the making of organs; their representative could hardly fail to appreciate the importance of instrumental manufacture to his home district, and to the nation as a whole.

When he accepted this assignment, Berlioz wrote that he would do his best to justify the Minister's confidence, and to "defend the French exhibitors" to the extent that the interests of art and the value of their work permitted. On leaving for London, on 9 May 1851, he wrote to Auguste Morel of the honor he felt such a mission entailed, and of his "astonishment" that in fact he had been asked to serve. His delight turned to dismay, however, as the task of auditioning so many wind and brass instruments gradually became more and more tiresome. But London, the Crystal Palace, and the Cathedral of Saint Paul's provided delights of many kinds – so much so that Berlioz stayed on an extra two weeks in order to finish the task as he believed it should be done. He later felt regret at having done so, for the administration long failed to reimburse his expenses in the English capital, and for a man who was as methodical about his personal finances as he was about his public obligations, this was painful. "Please be so good as to send me a full accounting, carefully explained, of my debts and obligations," he wrote to Adèle's husband, Marc Suat, on 25 October of that year; "I am very anxious to know exactly where I stand." Two weeks later he urged his brother-in-law to "neglect nothing" in the effort to extricate him from what was a momentary but serious cash-flow crisis.

Still, the superior qualities of the French instrument makers at the fair in London had fueled his chauvinism and boosted his morale. As the sole French member of the jury (otherwise composed of four Englishmen, two Germans, one Austrian, and one American), he seemed happy to conclude, in the official report, that the nation currently producing the finest musical instruments was France. To Joseph d'Ortigue he confided the same message: "It is France that has been victorious, without comparison, over all of Europe," he wrote on 21 June 1851; "All the others [. . .] produce only pots and pans, whistles and matchboxes."

Berlioz returned to London in the spring of 1852, when he was appointed conductor of the recently established New Philharmonic Society, and he gave a triumphant series of six concerts that culminated with Beethoven's Ninth Symphony. Back in Paris in the autumn, he directed the fourth complete performance of the *Requiem*, on 22 October, under the aegis of the Association des artistes musiciens – one of the momentous successes of his career (and the last time he gave the work in full). As always, he had had to obtain special approval from the directors of the government-supported theaters and of the Conservatoire, whose singers and musicians needed permission to perform *ex casa*. The director of the Opéra, Nestor Roqueplan, refused to allow his leading tenor (Gustave Roger) to take part, and Berlioz had to take the emergency measure of having the solo part in the *Sanctus* sung by four ordinary tenors – hardly a satisfactory choice (but one Berlioz unfortunately sanctioned with a note in the published score).

Why did Roqueplan deny Roger permission to sing for Berlioz? Was he really the ungrateful and hypocritical Philistine that Berlioz portrays in chapter 57 of the *Mémoires?* Was he opposed to the principles of the sponsoring Association des artistes? Roqueplan came from an artistic family (his brother was a successful painter) and, before coming to the Opéra, he had been a popular drama critic and a director of three lesser Parisian theaters; he was furthermore known as a highly spirited fellow and a master of the *bon mot.* Berlioz tells us that it was he – Berlioz himself – who, by exerting influence upon the Bertin family, had had Roqueplan named co-director of the Opéra in 1847. He also tells us that Roqueplan immediately reneged upon his promise to name Berlioz co-conductor of the orchestra there – yet another official post *manqué.* If Berlioz's influence was so great as to cause the authorities to name Roqueplan director at the Opéra, would it not have been sufficient to cause them to name him conductor at the same establishment? There is something oddly contradictory about Berlioz's account of this incident, and it would be fascinating to have the other side of the story. Nestor Roqueplan is one of those embodiments of officialdom – I spoke of them in the Introduction – from whom it would be instructive to hear more.

Berlioz returned yet again to London in 1853, where he gave a revised *Benvenuto Cellini* at Covent Garden, on 25 June. Though apparently very well performed, the opera fell victim to a cabal of hissing and disruption from a "well-disciplined band of malcontents," as *The Atlas* put it, motivated by an antipathy for anything that was not of purely Italian extraction: *Cellini* had been sung in Italian, as that house required, but Berlioz was not Bellini, and there were too many "foreigners" in the cast. Clearly hurt by such hostile behavior, Berlioz withdrew the work on the following day – rather too hastily, it seems to me, for the descriptions we have of the event suggest that a bit of perseverance (such as Diaghilev showed, half a century later, after the riotous première of *Le Sacre du printemps*) might well have overcome an opposition whose bark was inversely proportional to its bulk.

In 1854, Berlioz once more took to the road, this time not to

London, but rather to Hanover, Brunswick, and Dresden, where there was discussion of his taking over the post of chapel-master to the King of Saxony – the very post that Richard Wagner had occupied, under Reissiger, from 1843 until his forced exile as an active conspirator in the revolutionary uprisings of 1849. After two fine performances of *La Damnation de Faust* in Dresden, "the most magnificent rendering I have ever achieved for this difficult work," he told Liszt, Berlioz stopped briefly in Weimar before returning to Paris in early May.

In the summer of 1854 Berlioz completed two works, the cantata *L'Impériale* (which would enjoy a grand performance in the year to come), and the biblical oratorio that was to offer him the most immediate success of his entire career. After the failure of *Faust* in Paris in 1846, Berlioz had vowed never to "stake even twenty francs on the approval of his music by an audience in Paris." But as he later noted in the *Mémoires* (in a passage written in 1858), he failed to keep his vow:

> After having completed *L'Enfance du Christ*, I could simply not resist the temptation of having this work performed in Paris. Its success was immediate, and tremendous, so much so that it was positively insulting to my earlier compositions. I therefore gave it on several occasions in the Salle Herz; rather than ruining me, as had my performances of the *Damnation de Faust*, these actually brought me a profit of several thousand francs.

The sacred trilogy of *L'Enfance du Christ* – compiled from *Le Songe d'Hérode* (completed in July 1854), *La Fuite en Égypte* (drafted four years earlier, in 1850, and momentarily passed off as the work of the "seventeenth-century composer Pierre Ducré," whose name Berlioz had fashioned from that of his friend, the architect Joseph-Louis Duc), and *L'Arrivée à Saïs* (completed earlier in 1854) – was given twice in December 1854 and once in January 1855, always to tremendous applause. On the 11th of December – his fifty-first birthday, nine months after the death of Harriet Smithson, three weeks after his marriage to Marie Récio, and one day after the première of the new work –

Berlioz wrote to his brother-in-law that he had never been more warmly received, not in Germany, not in Russia, not in England. From Gounod, Adam, and Ambroise Thomas he received letters of congratulations, the last-named writing of the beauty of the form, color, and character of the work, and adding that "I know of nothing more profoundly impregnated with the poetry and tenderness of this admirable subject." Berlioz's reputation in France – to the extent that it had turned on accusations of bombast based on mis-information, mis-hearing, or misgiving in the face of dramatically motivated monumentality – was now reversed.

Berlioz made what turned out to be his last visit to London in June 1855, when he conducted concerts for the New Philharmonic Society to audiences "intoxicated with enthusiasm," for the English now considered him the world's greatest conductor. There he renewed his acquaintance with Richard Wagner, who was conducting for the Old Philharmonic Society. The two masters genuinely enjoyed each other's company as companions in misfortune ("Leidensgefährten" was Wagner's word), as admirers of Liszt, and as thinkers about music – although their communications were not always without difficulty. Indeed, Wagner would insightfully say that the language barrier would always keep the two of them apart: he spoke and sometimes wrote in French, but Berlioz – benefiting in his travels from the international predominance of his native tongue in political and cultural affairs – never learned German.

Their differences were more obviously manifest in the practical arena of orchestral conducting. Berlioz gained a reputation for especial fidelity to the composer's score, something confirmed by eye-witnesses' accounts as well as by the manual on conducting (commissioned by Alfred Novello) that he appended to the second edition of his treatise on orchestration. Wagner, on the other hand, became known as a conductor who took possession of a score and returned it to the public through the filter of his own imagination. Here is the prototype of the Toscanini–Furtwängler debate of earlier in the present century, and of the "authenticity" debate of the current era. At a distance of more than a century it is impossible to know what such notions as metronomic precision and *rubato* meant to Berlioz and Wagner, but I should think that both composers, like Mendelssohn when he first encountered the Société des Concerts du Conservatoire, were usually pleased simply to hear the right notes. Their encounter in the English capital is recounted in an informative and affectionate book, *Berlioz in London*, by A.W. Ganz, whose father, William, later a distinguished conductor, was one of Berlioz's regular London violinists.

Love, marriage, duty

At the beginning of the eighteen-forties, Berlioz had had little choice but to distance himself from his wife, irritated as he was by her surveillance, unable to meet her increasingly needy personal demands, frankly revolted by her excessive drinking, and beset with worries of his own. When Marie Récio became his traveling companion in 1842 and his domestic partner in 1844, Harriet could only have become more profoundly distressed. We can hear the loneliness she suffered in the letter she wrote to her son on 22 October 1846, after young Louis Berlioz had made a brief visit to Paris: "Your father hasn't come to see me since you left; he doesn't write to me, either. Tell me *everything* that he told you when you left – *everything, everything,* THE TRUTH." She must have known about Marie, but she clearly wanted to hear the details, in order to have the terrible satisfaction of confirming her darkest suspicions.

In October 1847 Harriet Smithson had the first of a series of strokes that led to partial paralysis, and she remained an invalid for the last four or five years of her life. Berlioz might have sent her to a sanitorium, but the idea of seeing her leave her warm garden for the chilly walls of an institution was as abhorrent to him as he knew it would be to her. The nomadic composer seems never to have failed to take care of her material necessities, as we know from various arrangements he made from abroad to have funds sent to his wife at home. He proclaimed to his family and friends that he could never abandon Harriet, but that it was simply impossible for him live regularly by her side. He suggests that Harriet would have found such closeness impossible as well, but we know nothing of her own view of the matter. By the time of her death, on 3 March 1854, she was unable even to speak. We may infer, from what Berlioz says about his sister Nanci, who died in 1850, that Harriet, too, raised as a child by a man who for forty years was a Pastor of the Church of Ireland, had at the end the comfort of thinking that she was about to enter the kingdom of heaven.

Berlioz's anguish on the death of his first wife was of the painfully nostalgic sort, filled with recollections of Shakespearean triumph and tragedy. But the event led him to order his life anew. In September 1854 he made a three-week trip to La Côte, partly to witness the execution of his father's will, and partly to inform his family that he intended to marry again. On Tuesday, 17 October 1854, having returned to the capital, Berlioz went with Marie and her mother to the office of his notary, Philippe-Athanase Beaufeu, in the rue Sainte-Anne, and signed a detailed contract of marriage. On Wednesday the 18th he completed and dated the last page of the last chapter of his *Mémoires* (which tells of Harriet's sad demise). On Thursday the 19th the couple went first to the Mairie of the second arrondissement, where a civil ceremony of marriage was performed, and then to the Église de la Trinité, in the rue de Clichy, where a religious ceremony took place. Among the four witnesses to the marriage was the London critic John Ella, who found the composer in much better spirits now that he had "only one wife to provide for."[7] Others present, I would guess, having found no official document, might have been Adolphe Sax, the instrument-maker, a good friend to both Berlioz and Marie and a witness as well to some of the required legalities when Marie died in 1862; Marie Métivier Mabille, of Noisy-le-Grand, who was Marie's god-daughter; Anne-Angéline Banderali, the daughter of Marie's voice teacher and one of her best friends; and Marie's mother, Maria Sotera de Villas.

A week after the ceremony, on 26 October, Berlioz wrote to his son with the news that his relationship with Marie Récio had now become permanent:

I have remarried. This protracted liaison, I know you will
understand, had become indissoluble. I could no less live alone than
I could abandon the person who had been living with me for fourteen
years. My uncle [Félix Marmion] was of this opinion, and was the
first to tell me as much during his last visit to Paris. All of my friends
thought likewise.

A parent who remarries can never fully predict the reaction of his or
her children to the "replacement" of a father or mother – thus the
apologetic tone of Berlioz's letter – but Louis, who had gone to sea
during the storms of his father's first marriage, accepted the news of
the second with equanimity, something that gave Berlioz real pleasure. The marriage contract itself spells out what Berlioz meant when
he told his son that his position would now be more "normal" and
more "acceptable," for it suggests that with Marie's possessions – not
only her jewelry, but her silver, her furniture, and her other abundant
household goods – the couple's life together could, in the new security of a legal relationship, be more openly comfortable.

Marie Récio has had bad press for over one hundred and fifty years.
Even today's eminent Berliozians find it difficult to show sympathy for
this little-known woman who was Berlioz's companion from 1840 or
1841, if not before, until her death in 1862. On the basis of pitifully
little information – comments made by Richard Wagner (that paragon
of virtue), Ernest Legouvé (not always reliable) and several others
including Berlioz himself (with his occasional tendency to exagger-
ate), she has generally been seen as untalented, unpleasant, and
somehow unworthy of her companion. In my view, it is foolish to
make her over into the pasteboard character of a shrew – as though
that were the only category available (apart from that of the angel). Is
not speaking of Marie Récio as a bore to cast doubt on Berlioz's own
character? Can we continue to think of him as sensitive, emotional,
intelligent, and deeply devoted to his friends, which he was, while
condemning her for being not passive clay in his hands, but overbearing, gossipy, and cruel? Here was a physically attractive woman
with something of the Mediterranean temperament of her mother

and, perhaps, something of the military bearing of her father, a woman who may well have radiated a strength different in kind from that of the subtly powerful and much admired women of the nineteenth-century salons (where wit prevailed) and therefore unappreciated by some in Berlioz's *entourage*. She appears to have been faithful to him as mistress and as wife, to have managed his household with efficiency, to have established a cordial relationship with his son, and to have showered affection upon his nieces. Indeed, Marie may have in some ways been more fit than Harriet to be a mother, and it is an unanswered question as to why she and Berlioz never produced a child. She was even aware of the possible acerbity of her character, and began her will with a request for forgiveness from those whom she might have caused distress.

After the marriage and in the remaining months of 1854, Berlioz was occupied with the preparations for the Christmastide performances of *L'Enfance du Christ*, which caused his good reputation to be born again. In February of the new year he traveled to Weimar, where Franz Liszt, a permanent resident there since 1848, had made the city of Goethe and Schiller into a welcoming locale for the execution of modern music. Berlioz had visited Weimar in 1843 and had returned in 1852 for performances of *Benvenuto Cellini* in a new version, cut to the specifications of the Grand-Ducal Theater and sponsored by the Grand Duchess, to whom Berlioz wrote a formal but very touching letter of gratitude. Now, in 1855, he gave two concerts of which the second – a benefit for the musicians' pension fund – included the new *L'Enfance du Christ* and the *Symphonie fantastique* with a revised *Retour à la vie*, both performed in Peter Cornelius's German translation. And he renewed his acquaintance with Liszt's mistress (since 1847), the Polish Princess Carolyne Sayn-Wittgenstein, who soon became an inspiration to Berlioz for the composition of *Les Troyens*.

In the autumn, after further travels to Brussels and, as we have seen, to London, Berlioz was appointed to the musical instrument jury for the Exposition Universelle of 1855. This was France's answer

12   A photographic portrait of Berlioz made for a *carte de visite*, *ca.* 1855, by
Gaspard-Félix Tournachon, known as Nadar.

to the London extravaganza of 1851, held in a new Palais de l'Industrie (on the site of today's Grand Palais) designed to advertise the economic prosperity of the growing French empire, and at a nearby Palais des Beaux-Arts designed to show that the régime wished not only to include but also to embrace the arts. (The huge retrospective exhibition of that year canonized Ingres, crowned Delacroix, and, by excluding him, pointed to Courbet as the giant of the future.) At first pleased to have been selected for the Commission of Inquiry, because in the art world the crowning of the victors was a much sought after privilege, Berlioz soon found the wages to be inadequate, as he had in 1851: for the enormous task of comparing the virtues of hundreds of pianos, harmoniums, melodiums, and brass and wind instruments of all kinds, he received little more, he tells us, than a crust of bread and a glass of wine at some official table.

In fact his real compensation came this time in the form of an imperial request to prepare several concerts for the Exposition's award ceremonies and closing festivities. He gave five truly "monster" concerts between 15 and 25 November 1855, three of which featured performances of the cantata he had completed one year earlier, first called *Le Dix Décembre* (to mark the anniversary of the date on which Louis Napoleon was elected President of the Republic), but soon renamed *L'Impériale* in accordance with the title of the poem that he actually set, a glorification of the Napoleonic dynasty penned by a career military officer, one Achille Lafon.

This monumental *œuvre de circonstance*, for two choruses and large orchestra, was conceived in terms well suited to the vast forces required to bring it to life – no fewer than seven hundred singers and five hundred players – and to the vast exhibition hall in which some thirty thousand dignitaries and guests were assembled for the formal announcement of the prizes. Subsequent concerts featured the *Apothéose* from the *Symphonie funèbre et triomphale* and four movements of the *Te Deum* (which had been given its first complete performance, at Saint-Eustache, only seven months earlier). The press reports on the ceremonies were eulogistic, and Berlioz's profits of some eight thousand francs were by any measure enormous. As the director of music for these epoch-making entertainments, and as the single living French composer represented on four of the five programs given before the myriads from home and abroad who had come to witness this exaltation of the Emperor and his capital, Berlioz has to be seen as having enjoyed a climactic moment in his career. The following year, on 18 August 1856, in gratitude for *L'Impériale*, Napoleon III offered him a gold medal that was worth five hundred francs.[8]

The irresistible Institut de France

In August of 1854, Berlioz had canceled a projected concert tour in Germany because he had learned that a chair was available in the Académie des Beaux-Arts of the Institut de France as a result of Fromental Halévy's decision to relinquish his seat in the music section in order to become Perpetual Secretary of the Academy as a whole. Berlioz spent a week paying short visits to all the members of the Academy in order to present his credentials and to ask for support, as the time-honored custom required all candidates to do. But he was soon passed over by the so-called "immortals" in favor of the composer Louis Clapisson, well known at the time from his works for the Opéra and Opéra Comique and from his dedication to the singing societies of the Orphéon movement. One day after the voting, on 27 August 1854, Berlioz explained to his sister Adèle why he had wished to enter the lists:

> The position is worth 1,500 francs, that's the whole of it. But for me, that is a lot. I will say nothing of the honor involved, for this is surely a fiction, considering those who now compose and who have always composed the membership. I have so far presented my candidacy on only two occasions [in 1842 and 1851]. Hugo had to knock on the door some five times, De Vigny four. Eugène Delacroix, after six successive attempts, has still not been able to pry it open, and *De Balzac* never did get in. And yet the place is a den of fools . . .

It had long been Berlioz's habit to denigrate the "fools" of the Institute, ever since the years during which he was competing for the

Prix de Rome, when his original cantatas were rejected by the judges in favor of more conventional compositions by composers all of whom are now forgotten. He became quite expert on the rules of the *concours* and wrote about them, always with sarcasm, in his column. And yet, as early as 1839, it was suggested in the press that he be named to the Academy, when a *fauteuil* became vacant due to the death of Ferdinand Paër. When Gasparo Spontini expressed the desire to be elected, however, some seem to have suspended their candidacies as a sign of respect for the esteemed composer of *La Vestale*. In fact Berlioz made no official application in 1839, but Adolphe Adam, who did, eventually withdrew in favor of the celebrated Italian composer, at the time court composer to Frederick William III and director of the opera house in Berlin. In order to accept election to the Institut de France, Spontini had to become a naturalized Frenchman, as the rules required, and he had to *reside in Paris*.[9] That he accepted to do so suggests a respect for the institution rather greater than what his longtime admirer, Berlioz, purported to feel.

When Cherubini died in 1842, Berlioz did present an official letter of candidacy that listed all his works and accomplishments, but Georges Onslow was elected. When Spontini himself died, in 1851, Berlioz applied again, but Ambroise Thomas got the nod. And, as we have seen, in 1854, he made a third attempt, only to be edged out by Clapisson. Finally, when Adolphe Adam died, on 3 May 1856, Berlioz, now known as the composer of the successful oratorio, *L'Enfance du Christ*, sent yet another letter of candidacy to the president of the Académie des Beaux-Arts, made two rounds of visits to the thirty-nine members of the larger group, and eventually learned, to his delight, on 21 June 1856, that he had been elected.

I have always found a certain inconsistency in accounts of Berlioz's efforts to become a member of the nation's highest academic fraternity, including his own. If the honor was so trivial as he suggests, why did he – and the others mentioned here, by no means all of whom were deprived of financial resources – continue assiduously to attempt to pry the doors open, to use Berlioz's image regarding Delacroix (who

13 The façade of the Institut de France, from *Picturesque Architecture in Paris, Ghent, Antwerp, Rouen, etc., drawn from nature on stone by Thomas Shotter Boys, 1839* (reprint: London, 1928).

did gain entrance on his *seventh* attempt)? Indeed, some of the letters Berlioz wrote at the time of the 1856 vote suggest to me that he literally hungered for victory. When it came, his greatest pleasure seems magnanimously to have been that of providing an opportunity for his friends and family to be happy *for him*. But he must have understood the election as a kind of inscription into the collective memory of the nation – and so, too, did the larger musical public. Indeed, Berlioz's reputation could not help but be enhanced by this nomination, and it is probably the case that some of the gloom and doom that hangs over the *Mémoires* would have been lessened had their author entered the Institute before that book was in its final draft.

Berlioz obviously felt that the letters of congratulations which arrived from all quarters when the news of his nomination to the Institute became public were well worth safe keeping, for a good number of them survive.[10] Ernest Legouvé was the first to use the consecrated formula and address his old friend as "illustre confrère"; Mme Lesueur wrote of how much her husband would have loved to have been able to sit at the Institute in the company of one of his beloved students; Jean de Bay – a friend of whose relationship with the composer we know nothing – sent the compliments of a "vieux camarade." Some read the news with disbelief, and took it as a "triumph" for art, as justice belatedly rendered, as rectification long overdue. Frederick Beale and John Ella cheered him from London; like so many others, they took the news as an honor not only for Berlioz, not only for the Institute, but for the nation of France as a whole. From the Princess Wittgenstein, he received the congratulations of "all Weimar," and from the Countess of Mniszech (the daughter of Balzac's widow, Mme Hanska), the regret that Balzac had not lived long enough to witness Berlioz's achievement. Even Berlioz's old enemy, F.-J. Fétis, sent a word of congratulations, to which Berlioz replied with good humor: "I am really very glad that you are not too angry at the Institute for what happened at the last election." On the Saturday immediately following his nomination, 28 June 1856, Berlioz joined his five new *confrères* – Auber, Carafa, Thomas, Reber, and Clapisson (who was succeeded by Charles Gounod in 1866) – to begin what became twelve and a half years of "academic" work.

Berlioz soon put to use the newly elevated stature and limited favor he now enjoyed in princely circles when, in July 1857, he urged the Emperor to bestow the medal of the Légion d'honneur upon the organ manufacturer Édouard Alexandre. Written to honor a friend and generous benefactor (who would purchase a plot in the cemetery of Montmartre for Berlioz's family, in 1862), the following letter (not included in Berlioz's collected correspondence; reproduced here in illustration 14) expresses a pride in French industry that we can be certain is sincere:

> Sire
> Charged by Your Majesty's government with studying the industrial production of other nations as a member of the Commission of Inquiry, I have been able to observe the importance of various European manufacturers in the production of musical instruments and France's now incontestable superiority in this special area of endeavor.
>
> This superiority is due in particular to M. Édouard Alexandre, on whose behalf representatives of our principal musical institutions have already addressed a request to His Excellency the Minister of Commerce similar to that which I now presume to address to Your Majesty.
>
> Forgive me, Sire, for taking the liberty, with respect, of requesting for him the decoration of the Legion of Honor as the most powerful consecration of his success and the most excellent encouragement of his efforts. This ingenious manufacturer already employs six hundred workers; he is without doubt the most celebrated representative of this branch of French industry.
>
> I am, with the deepest respect, Sire, for Your Majesty,
> the very humble and very obedient servant and subject,
> Hector Berlioz
> Membre de l'Institut, etc.[11]

What is noteworthy here, what may suggest some particular familiarity, is that while the others who supported the organ manufacturer wrote to the then Minister of Commerce, Eugène Rouher, Berlioz sent his recommendation (which proved to be successful) directly to Napoleon III.

Did membership in the Institute make any significant difference in bringing Berlioz's music, notably *Les Troyens*, to performance in Paris? The short answer is no, for what should have been taken up *in toto* by the Opéra was in fact put on only five years later, in a partial version, at the Théâtre Lyrique, as we shall see below. Still, in his later years, Berlioz always enjoyed the stroll down to the Louvre and across the river to the Palais de l'Institut, where the meetings of the Académie des Beaux-Arts took place under the gracious dome designed by Le Vau in the mid-seventeenth century. (The building was accessible to those who lived on the right bank of the Seine by the pedestrian Pont des Arts, constructed by Napoleon in the year of Berlioz's birth.) The Academy, whose current membership of forty (fourteen painters, eight sculptors, eight architects, four engravers, six composers) was shaped during the Restoration, under Louis XVIII, is best known for issuing the Prix de Rome, but its members were also called upon to review monographs and dissertations, to evaluate instruments and *méthodes*, to serve on special commissions, and to deliberate upon the individual entries of a *Dictionnaire général des beaux-arts*, which began to appear in 1859. As a whole it represented the embodiment of a national concern to inventory the state of mankind's general knowledge, to maintain respect for aesthetic tradition, and to elucidate that greatly prized if highly elusive quality of *bon goût*.

By my calculation, during the nearly thirteen years of his tenure at the Institute, Berlioz attended over three hundred and sixty meetings of the Academy – an average of one meeting every two weeks in the years between 1856 and 1869 – something that suggests, despite his mockery of the place, that he actually enjoyed and felt responsible to this now venerable institution. The pose he struck in what became his preferred photographic portrait (see illustration 15 on p. 164) is certainly of the deliberative sort appropriate to an honored academician.

In the spring of 1862, when Fromental Halévy died, Berlioz's

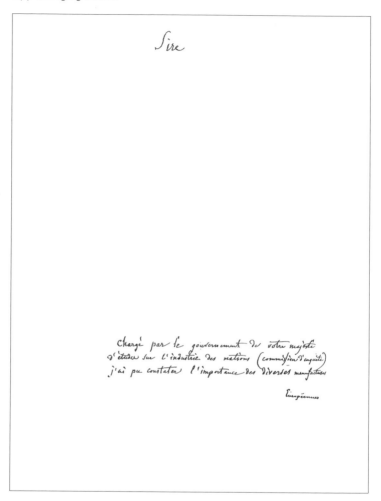

14 Berlioz's letter to Napoleon III, of July 1857, requesting the decoration of the Légion d'honneur for Édouard Alexandre.

fellows urged him to become a candidate for the post of Perpetual Secretary, which Halévy had held since 1854. The job carried with it free lodgings at the Institute, no small perquisite in a town where renting an apartment has never been inexpensive, but the tasks of writing and editing reports and *éloges* for recently deceased colleagues, for which he was eminently qualified, had little appeal for Berlioz. He was

Européennes dans la production des instruments de
musique, et la supériorité maintenant incontestable
de la France dans cette spécialité.

Ce résultat est dû surtout à M. Edouard Alexandre,
pour lequel les représentants de nos principales institutions
musicales ont déjà fait à Son Excellence M. le ministre du
commerce une demande semblable à celle que j'ose
adresser à votre majesté.

Pardonnez moi, Sire, de prendre la respectueuse
liberté de demander pour lui la décoration de
la légion d'honneur, comme la plus haute consécration
de ses succès et l'encouragement le plus puissant de
ses efforts. Cet ingénieux manufacturier occupe déjà
plus de six cents ouvriers ; il est certainement le
plus célèbre représentant de cette branche de l'industrie
française.

Je suis avec le plus profond
respect

Sire

De votre majesté
le très humble et très obéissant serviteur
et sujet
Hector Berlioz
membre de l'Institut etc

content to participate as a regular member of the fraternity, to rub
elbows with the painters and architects as well as the composers, and,
with his exalted visiting card marked simply *Membre de l'Institut*, to frequent the Emperor Napoleon (whose temperature of "twenty-five
degrees below zero," Berlioz quipped, usually rendered him inaccess-
ible) and the Empress Eugénie (whom, by contrast, he always found

charming). The card ensured treatment with respect; the job, a bracing weekly routine, and friendly and pleasant relations during what was often a physically and psychologically painful old age.

Dido, Beatrice, Shakespeare, and Marie

It is fitting that Berlioz's two final operas should derive from the contrasting sources of classical antiquity, on the one hand, and Shakespeare, on the other. Their separate virtues of freedom and restraint were the stuff of the great aesthetic debates of his youth – the subjects of Stendhal's *Racine et Shakespeare* (1823) and Hugo's *Préface de Cromwell* (1827), among other pamphlets, and the reason behind the *bataille d'Hernani* (1830) that marked the dawn of the romantic era in France. Berlioz's music of the eighteen-thirties may have been in a new mode for what was widely perceived as a new age – but his lukewarm appreciation of *Hernani* itself was a signal of the classicizing bent that was never totally absent from his creative imagination, and that found fulfillment in the work that crowns the tradition of French Grand Opera, *Les Troyens*.

The catalogue of Berlioz's work includes notice of at least eleven operas that were "contemplated but not composed" – the result of the character of his musical talents and the strain of his relationships with the administrators who controlled the Opéra. After the disappointment of *Benvenuto Cellini* in 1838 and 1839, Berlioz did complete three acts of a five-act grand opera, *La Nonne sanglante* (on a libretto by Eugène Scribe and Germain Delavigne), between 1841 and 1847, but he then abandoned the subject, which was eventually taken over by Charles Gounod and premiered at the Opéra in 1854. The vicissitudes of the Parisian operatic world were obviously clear to Berlioz when he yielded to overmastering artistic necessity and determined to write *Les Troyens*, in full knowledge that the prospects were dim for seeing an opera based on Virgil's *Aeneid* produced on the Parisian stage. Operatic subjects from antiquity had not been common since the period of the Revolution and the First Empire – but the opposition Berlioz feared was not to Virgil, of course, but to his modern champion.

He began in the Wagnerian manner, by drafting the libretto himself, in the spring of 1856, taking up the tales of the Virgilian demigods who had moved him since his childhood, and shaping them into a series of *tableaux* (destined for eventual setting in a series of musical numbers) that portray – via retrospective narration, predictive recital, and action on the stage – the Trojan people's misguided reception of the famous wooden horse, the entrusting to Aeneas of the treasures of the city of Troy as its walls fall to the Greeks, the arrival of the Trojans at Carthage in self-congratulatory celebration, the ignition of the passion between Queen Dido and the valiant Trojan leader, and the terrible disintegration of the world of the lovers as fate summons Aeneas to Rome. Berlioz wrote with ease and excitement because his own dreams of distant adventure had been always inspired by the great Latin poet: Virgil, he wrote in the second chapter of the *Mémoires* (drafted only a few years earler, in the spring of 1848), "in speaking to me of epic passions which I had at the time [of my childhood] only just begun to understand, was the first to find the way to my heart and to inflame my budding imagination." With its use of classical alexandrines, mid-line caesuras, prepositioned adjectives, and regular rhymes, the French text that Berlioz completed by the end of June (and that he discussed in detail with the Princess Wittgenstein, who always encouraged him to persevere) is clearly touched by archaisms apt to the suggestion of Imperial Rome. But in moments of great emotion – such as the death of Dido (where Berlioz's personal copy of the *Aeneid*, which has been preserved, is most worn) – the poetry breathes the unrestrained rhythms of real human emotion.

Before setting down the notes, he wrote to the Princess that what he hoped to create was the sort of music that she herself called "free":

> To find the means of being *expressive* and *truthful* without musical sacrifice, to find the way, rather, of giving the music itself new instruments of action – *that* is the problem.

He worked methodically and excitedly through 1857 (via correspondence we can follow his progress in intimate detail), he built a five-act grand opera of noble proportion (roughly equivalent in length to that of the principal operas of Meyerbeer, and not the elongated monstrosity of his enemies' imaginations), and he dated the last bar of the score 12 April 1858. For the next five years, as he struggled to bring the work to life, Berlioz continued to make revisions, small and large, in accordance with the exigencies of potential performance and publication. It is easy to equate those struggles with failure, but even as he was completing the score, he felt, as he told Adolphe Samuel on 26 February 1858, that whether *Les Troyens* was performed was in fact of little importance: his "musical and Virgilian passions" had been satisfied, and he had demonstrated what he believed could be done "with an antique subject treated on a grand scale."

In this imposing work, whose libretto is rich with literal echoes from the *Aeneid* and whose imperial design seems in harmony with the then national order, the inspiration of that other giant in his pantheon, Shakespeare, makes itself felt in a quite specific way, and in a scene that encapsulates one of the supreme moments of the drama. When writing the poetry of the impassioned exchange between Dido and Aeneas that forms the concluding duet of the penultimate act of the opera, Berlioz took over the strophic form of the scene between Jessica and Lorenzo at the opening of Act 5 of *The Merchant of Venice*; he took over the literary conceit of persistent comparison, the third-person self-references, and even the ironic note of forgiveness that punctuates the lovers' exchange. The repeated invocation of the lovely "In such a night," in Shakespeare, and the mention of the symbolic figure of Queen Dido –

> *Jessica*   In such a night
> Did Thisbe fearfully o'ertrip the dew,
> And saw the lion's shadow ere himself,
> And ran dismayed away.
> *Lorenzo*   In such a night
> Stood Dido with a willow in her hand
> Upon the wild sea banks, and waft her love
> To come again to Carthage.

– become, in Berlioz (where Dido is "real"), the repeated utterance "par une telle nuit":

Énée Par une telle nuit la pudique Diane
Laissa tomber enfin son voile diaphane
Aux yeux d'Endymion.
Didon Par une telle nuit le fils de Cythérée
Accueillit froidement la tendresse enivrée
De la reine Didon!

(Aeneas On such a night the modest Diana
Let fall at last her gauzy veil
Before the eyes of Endymion.
Dido On such a night the son of Cytherea[12]
Responded coldly to the impassioned tenderness
Of Queen Dido.)

The similarities and differences here are highly instructive, for Berlioz has made of Shakespeare's blank verse the strictly rhymed poetry characteristic of the traditional operatic libretto, writing two pairs of three lines – with a rhyme scheme of aab/ccb – of which the first two are classical alexandrines of twelve syllables, the third a half-line of six. Shakespeare's Jessica and Lorenzo conclude their conversation on a playful note: Lorenzo mockingly accuses his love of "slander," for which he forgives her; and Jessica, after hearing "in such a night" for the fourth time (she has herself uttered it thrice), replies that "I would out-night you, did nobody come; but hark, I hear the footing of a man" – at which point a messenger arrives, and the happy conclusion unfolds. No such happy conclusion is possible in Les Troyens, of course, for the hero, emotionally torn, is predestined to choose duty over love.

To round out his formal scheme in the duet, Berlioz surrounds the "par une telle nuit" verses with a refrain whose exquisite first line, "Nuit d'ivresse et d'extase infinie," inspired a melody of elegant simplicity, with an especially graceful flourish for the final e of the word infinie. (Unheard in speech, the final mute e must be sounded separately when sung, in accordance with a rule of French prosody

that is responsible for the larger coherence of all *mélodie française*.) We hear "par une telle nuit" only four times, which is too few to have one of the lovers charmingly attempt to "out-night" the other. And the irony of forgiveness, as Aeneas pardons Dido for her "unjust" accusations, is here not playful, for the lovers are doomed to separation – as we learn from the appearance at the end of the scene of the messenger, the god Mercury, who gestures toward the sea and cries out "Italie!" (four syllables), admonishing Aeneas to pursue his fated and ultimate destination.

The appearance of Mercury consummates in a highly dramatic way what is arguably the most astonishingly beautiful expanse of music that Berlioz ever wrote: the passage in Act 4 that stretches from the quintet (No. 35), in which Dido, hearing Aeneas's tale, begins to allow the memory of her husband to subside and her love of Aeneas to swell, through the sextet (No. 36), in which Aeneas urges all to set aside sad memories and breathe in the splendors of the night, to the duet (No. 37), in which the protagonists rapturously declaim their love in literally Shakespearean verse. We know from correspondence that Berlioz could not resist setting down the music of the duet, even before he completed the poem (the only instance of such a "transgression"), so intoxicated had he become with this ultimate dramatic moment, which he referred to as Virgil *Shakespearianisé*. He chose the key of G flat major – the same remote key in which Meyerbeer had composed the love duet of *Les Huguenots* (1836) and Halévy that of *La Reine de Chypre* (1841), and the only extended music that Berlioz ever wrote in that ever distant key (which Richard Wagner took up, too, for one of his own exercises in sublimity, the quintet in Act 3 of *Die Meistersinger*). The premonitory appearance of Mercury, at the moment the lovers have receded into the distance, is accentuated by what is a *harmonic* twist of fate, for it shatters the promise of domestic tranquillity, and leaves us in E minor, almost as far from the bliss of G flat major as the world of tonality would allow.

The world of the Paris Opéra was equally far from blissful, for Berlioz, and negotiations for a performance of his new musical epic at

that theater (where he had successfully provided recitatives for *Der Freischütz*, in 1841, and where he would successfully supervise revivals of Gluck's *Alceste*, in 1861 and again in 1866) blew more cold than hot. Had Napoleon III had a greater interest in music, *Les Troyens* would have had a happier fate. But the Emperor was more interested in public transportation than in music (it was under Napoleon III that the French railway system was fully established), and he had an especial concern for city planning: the Baron Haussmann became Prefect of the Seine during his reign, in 1853, and began then to work the miracle of reconstruction that soon made Paris the most beautiful city in the world. It happens that at the most important crossroads of Haussmann's grand design was an opera house – the "Palais Garnier" as we now know it (after its architect, Charles Garnier) – an edifice whose functional iron superstructure was at the time of its construction as modern as its decorative stone façade was traditional. Here was a theatrical sign of imperial patronage and a symbol of the nation that was surpassed only a generation later, when Gustave Eiffel built an iron tower to commemorate the one-hundredth anniversary of the Great Revolution of 1789.

The Garnier opera house was only completed six years after Berlioz's death, and five years after Napoleon III's demise, in 1875. It opened not with *Les Troyens*, but with excerpts from Halévy's *La Juive* (1835) and Meyerbeer's *Les Huguenots* (1836), along with Leo Delibes' ballet *La Source* (1866). Well before the new Opéra was even underway, Berlioz had tried at length to interest the Emperor in his Virgilian epic. He summarized the situation to Liszt in a letter of 28 September 1858:

> The Emperor told me to bring him the libretto [of *Les Troyens*], having accorded me an audience that I thought was to be private. But there were forty-two of us, and it was impossible for me to say more than a few words to him. With that air of his that registers twenty-five degrees below zero, he took my manuscript and assured me that he would read it, *if he could find a moment of leisure to do so*. Since then I have heard nothing.

Nor did he ever hear from the Emperor about Les Troyens, which was eventually put on not at the Opéra, and not in full, but at the Théâtre Lyrique, and, as we shall see, hewn in half. Berlioz's support of Napoleon III, based on hopeful visions of imperial enlightenment, appears not to have worked to his advantage in the most critical engagement of his late maturity. Of the French Emperor Berlioz might have repeated what he had said in 1852 to Alexey Lvov, director of the Russian Imperial Chapel, about the Czar Nicholas I: "Quel malheur qu'il n'aime pas la musique!" – "What a shame that he doesn't like music!"

It was in January of 1860 – as pressure from imperial circles caused the Opéra to turn to Wagner's Tannhäuser – that Berlioz signed a contract to have Les Troyens produced at the new Théâtre Lyrique. The director there, Léon Carvalho, had employed Berlioz in 1859, to prepare and supervise a production of Gluck's Orphée, with Pauline Viardot in the title role, and he was enthusiastic about Berlioz's similarly classic music drama. But a series of administrative permutations soon took place at both the Théâtre Lyrique and the Opéra, and plans to mount Les Troyens ricocheted between them for some three years before finally coming to rest at the smaller house, where the composer was persuaded, because of limited resources, to give only the Cathaginian acts of his noble, five-act creation. Thus it was – to say in three words what requires three thousand – that Les Troyens became La Prise de Troie (the original Acts 1 and 2, which were never performed during Berlioz's lifetime) and Les Troyens à Carthage (the original Acts 3, 4, and 5, variously cut and compromised), which were premiered at the Lyrique on 4 November 1863.

Berlioz often expressed love for the heroines of his opera, the cursed prophetess Cassandra, whom he had crafted from only a few lines in Virgil, and the grief-stricken Queen Dido, but if he had any real amorous adventures in the wake of his second marriage, we are not informed of them. He seems to have settled into a businesslike arrangement with Marie, and to have managed their pecuniary

resources with care. Dozens of small financial memoranda, preserved in various collections, give us evidence of his systematical
behavior:

> I left 300 francs with my mother-in-law and I am taking with me 500
> francs in gold, leaving in my bag, which is in the right-hand drawer
> of my table: (1) a voucher for 1,000 francs payable at my convenience
> by Édouard Alexandre; (2) a bank note for 100 francs; (3) 340 francs
> in gold; (4) 40 francs in silver; (5) a roll of 118 francs. Total left in my
> drawer in Paris: 1,598 francs. In addition, I have 259 francs in State
> annuities in a box enclosed in the mirrored armoire in the
> bedroom.[13]

In the days before checking accounts and credit cards, squirreling
away cash in the nooks and crannies of one's apartment was not
uncommon. But this sort of jotting, when joined to his other monetary lamentations, sometimes causes us to see Berlioz as a nearly
ruined character out of a story by Balzac, or to feel as though we our-
selves are going through bankruptcy with him, with death – in the
form of the debt-collector – about to knock at both our doors. In fact
the death of his parents eventually provided Berlioz with a slender but
lasting blanket of financial security. When his mother died, on 8
March 1838, he came into an income of twelve hundred francs per
year, and when his father died, on 28 July 1848, he inherited an income
of six thousand francs annually along with four properties in his
native department of the Isère. When his father's estate was finally
disbursed, in 1854, Berlioz's financial situation was permanently sta-
bilized.

Reading the letters of that year, seeing the regularization of his
union with Marie, the renewal of gratifying relations with his son, and
the renaissance of his career after the success of *L'Enfance du Christ*, one
is tempted to say that, for a time, even into the period of *Les Troyens*,
Berlioz was both happy and economically secure. Only a few years earlier, for example, Richard Wagner thought that he could work without
the anxiety of having to "earn" his living with an income of *three* thousand francs per annum, which his admirers Julie Ritter and Jessie

Laussot proposed to offer the German composer in 1849 – yet Berlioz's income was now at least three times that amount, and sometimes more.

Despite a measure of financial security, the couple's relationship was not without its storms. For example, in 1858 Berlioz had to act to prevent Marie from losing money on the stock exchange by writing to a financial agent:

> If it should happen that despite my prohibition, Mme Berlioz, my wife, should wish to speculate on the market, and for this purpose address herself to your good offices, I must inform you in advance that I will recognize none of the debts she might incur in this way.[14]

This admonition could represent the tip of a sinister iceberg. But we have no further evidence of it, for in most of Berlioz's later correspondence, he reports on Marie to his friends and family with the polite formulas regarding her health that suggest nothing other than genuine affection and concern.

Indeed, on the emotional roller coaster that finally led to a production of *Les Troyens*, Marie amply shared Berlioz's ups and downs. She certainly shared his satisfaction at the failure of the work that had blocked Berlioz's path to the Opéra. In public, Berlioz had remained honorably silent about the failure of Wagner's *Tannhäuser*, turning his column in the *Débats* over to his faithful colleague Joseph d'Ortigue. Still, his demeanor revealed his thoughts, as he sat in his loge at the Opéra,

> wrapped in his high-buttoned coat, with that remarkable head of his proudly perched atop a neck that was bound in a silken black cravat in the style of the eighteen-thirties, looking like a bird of prey, with his imposing forehead buried under a mass of thick gray hair, his eyes piercing, and his lips twisted in a malicious grin.[15]

Marie, to Wagner's eventual displeasure, apparently voiced her feelings more openly. We find a hint of her chatter in the letter she wrote to Berlioz's nieces Joséphine and Nanci Suat, on 20 March 1861, one week after the première of *Tannhäuser*, in which she mentions that Paris had been lately deluged by squalls:

> But the worst storm, this one entirely terrestrial, is the one we had at the Opéra on Wednesday the 13th. None of the subscribers can remember such a total *failure*, one that was, I have to admit, entirely deserved. M. Wagner now has good reason to regret having used *imperial authority* in order to climb over the backs of everyone else, for he has fallen flat on his face, and has been buried under all the hooting and laughter. The second performance was even more tempestuous than the first; the third has not yet been announced. The Emperor was present at both performances and was able to witness in person the maneuvers of his French comrades. And he himself was laughing [. . .] Now we are finally free from that whole clique of the *music of the future*, or at least I should like to think we are, after such a brutal confrontation.[16]

Such emotional support must have comforted the composer, whose reaction we can scarcely imagine had he found that the woman who shared his bed was a Wagnerian. None the less, more than one observer has taken it as a kind of muted comeuppance that Berlioz's second wife is alluded to only twice in his *Mémoires*, and never by name. This is to forget, I think, that Berlioz's volume, unlike those of Rousseau and Chateaubriand, does not provide a chronological traversal of his career, at a constant tempo, from beginning to end. Only three-quarters of his life, from youth to age fifty-one, occupy the *Mémoires*, while his last fifteen years – the period of *Les Troyens* and *Béatrice et Bénédict* – are sketched with little detail. The obvious reason for this, apart from his literary desire to avoid play-by-play description and his personal desire to have done with the book, is that a truthful account of more recent times would touch not only Marie, but a number of individuals who were still alive. As for her: any writer would have been unwilling to alienate conventional readers by recording a relationship which, during its first fourteen years, was "immoral." And most writers would have preferred to set forth the dramatic actions of Harriet Smithson (whom Berlioz always thought of as

Ophelia) and Camille Moke (whom he early on dubbed Ariel, the bird-like spirit of *The Tempest*) rather than the doubtless competent activities of Marie Récio (whose prosaic person never led to a Shakespearean epithet). Berlioz's literary penchant explains why Camille Saint-Saëns later wondered, with some seriousness, "Was it really Camille and Harriet whom Berlioz loved? Or was it Ariel and Ophelia?"

It was while visiting her friends Pierre Orry de La Roche and his wife, in Saint-Germain-en-Laye, that Marie died of a heart attack, on the morning of 13 June 1862. Berlioz may well have told his son (a year earlier) that marriage was "the heaviest millstone that one can hang round one's neck," but the news of Marie's death disoriented him far more than had the news of Harriet's death twelve years before, for it was unexpected (though Marie had earlier had heart problems), and it struck him at the more advanced age of almost fifty-nine years. Little consoled by letters and visits from family and friends, and by the presence of his faithful mother-in-law, Berlioz suffered miserably from feelings of isolation, as he told Henry Vieuxtemps, for, since their marriage, neither he nor Marie had ever lived or traveled alone.

Berlioz had already had Marie buried when his friend Édouard Alexandre purchased for him a new funeral vault in the cemetery of Montmartre. This necessitated that he make arrangements for, and witness, her exhumation and re-interment. It then came about, by tragi-comical coincidence, that Berlioz's *first* wife would also have to be exhumed and re-interred, because of the demolition of another part of the same Montmartre cemetery. At the end of the Postface of the *Mémoires*, Berlioz described with near scientific precision the proceedings that he witnessed on that second grisly occasion (of 3 February 1864):

> A municipal officer assigned to observe the exhumation was waiting for me. The gravedigger had already opened the pit; when I arrived, he jumped down into it. The coffin, already ten years in the ground, was still intact, but the lid had been damaged by the dampness. Instead of lifting the whole coffin out of the ground, therefore, the gravedigger yanked up the rotting planks, which came away with a hideous noise as they left exposed the contents of the casket. The

gravedigger bent down and with his two hands picked up the head, already separated from the body – the ungarlanded, hairless, and sadly withered head of "poor Ophelia" – and placed it in a new coffin ready for it at the edge of the pit. Then, bending down again, he lifted with great difficulty and gathered into his arms the headless trunk and limbs, a blackish mass which the shroud still clung to, and which resembled a lump of pitch wrapped in a damp sac. There was a dull sound . . . and a terrible smell . . . The municipal officer, a few steps away, was observing this lugubrious tableau. Seeing me leaning back against a cypress tree, he called out, "Don't stay there M. Berlioz, come over here, come over here!" And as if the grotesque had also to have its part in this appalling scene, he added (mistaking the word), "Ah, poor *inhumanity!*" A few moments later, following the hearse that was transporting these sad remains, we went down the hill to the larger cemetery where the new vault was already wide open. Henriette's remains were laid in it. The two dead women now lie there in peace, awaiting the time when I shall bring to the same charnel house my own rotted carcass.

Fearing solitude after the death of Marie, Berlioz used to wander regularly in the cemetery of Montmartre, not far from his apartment. There he befriended a woman more than thirty years his junior, who, unbeknownst to Berlioz, was apparently mortally ill. We know nothing of her save that her name was Amélie, that she fell in love with Berlioz, and that after some hesitation he fell in love with her. A few months later, circumstances caused the lovers reluctantly to part. It was only by accident, on another stroll through the cemetery, that Berlioz discovered a grave "of whose opening and closing" he had been unaware. Amélie "had been dead for six months," he told the Princess Wittgenstein in August 1864, "and no one had thought or been able to tell me that she was dying. She was twenty-six years old, she was beautiful, and she wrote like an angel."

In the summers of 1853, 1856, and every summer thereafter through 1863, Berlioz gave concerts in the salons and theaters at Baden-Baden, the elegant spa across the Rhine from Strasburg, where the European rich and famous came to enjoy the casino, the attractions of the town, and the lovely south German landscape. Berlioz in Baden became one of the happier chapters of his life, and serves as a small corrective to those accounts that would accentuate only the despondency of his last decade. The manager of the casino there, Édouard Bénazet, was the "veritable sovereign" of the community, in Berlioz's words, and the force behind the artistic vitality of what was an internationally celebrated *festival estival* that became known to Brahms, Clara Schumann, and Wagner, to Turgenev and Dostoevsky, and to a host of others in the higher realms of politics and the arts. In 1858 Bénazet had the wisdom to commission Berlioz to write an opera for Baden's newly constructed theater, and after some hesitation the composer produced *Béatrice et Bénédict*, a two-act comic opera based on Shakespeare's *Much Ado About Nothing* that he had actually contemplated as early as 1833. The first performance of the opera took place on 9 August 1862, and six months later the vocal score was published with a sincere dedication to that generous master of summer ceremonies: "Without you," Berlioz wrote to Bénazet on 26 January 1863, this score "would simply not exist."

Of all Berlioz's heroes, Shakespeare seems most frequently, in his music as in his life, to have taken pride of place. From the early choral and orchestral *Fantaisie dramatique* on *The Tempest* of 1830, through the symphony on *Romeo and Juliet* (and the love scene of *Les Troyens*), and on to the taking over of *Much Ado About Nothing* for *Béatrice et Bénédict*, he was preoccupied with bringing Shakespearean passions, contrasts, and oppositions into sound. Berlioz consoled himself by reading the plays in private – he came to know almost all of them, and infused his correspondence with remembered quotations from passages both famous and obscure – and engrossed his friends by reading the plays in public. It is hardly surprising that when a *Comité shakespearien français* was organized to celebrate in Paris the three-hundredth anniversary of the birth of the bard, in 1864, its distinguished membership, along with George Sand, Émile Littré, Jules Michelet, Auguste Barbier, Alexandre Dumas, Théophile Gautier, Jules Janin, and a number of dignitaries from the world of politics and the arts – included that master of "bardolatry," Berlioz himself. (At the last minute, the banquet to memorialize the anniversary, scheduled for the 23rd of April, was banned by the government, which was fearful that the occasion – to be presided over by Victor Hugo *in absentia* – would be used as an expression of opposition to the Imperial Régime.)

Quotations from *Hamlet* and *Romeo and Juliet* serve as epigraphs for each of the movements of *Huit Scènes de Faust* of 1829, as though the English poet, whom Berlioz took to be the explicator of his own life, could also be the explicator of Goethe's drama. To view the Egyptian Queen contemplating suicide, in the *Méditation* that closes the prize cantata of the same year, *Cléopâtre*, Berlioz applied a quotation from the scene of Juliet at the tomb of the Capulets. Citations from Shakespeare also appear in the published nocturnal rondo of 1829, the *Ballet des ombres*, and in the manuscript of the *Fantastique*. In 1834 the idea of an opera based on *Hamlet* was floated in his direction, and while nothing came of it, Berlioz did complete, in 1842, the first of several versions of *La Mort d'Ophélie* based on Ernest Legouvé's ballad written "in imitation of Shakespeare"; in 1844 he thought of combining this with two further numbers as a suite of incidental music for a possible production of the tragedy. "Imité de Shakespeare" would have been the notation after the titles of two of the operas he momentarily dreamed about writing, on *Romeo and Juliet* and *Antony and Cleopatra*, in 1859, and it is the notation after the title of Berlioz's final opera, *Béatrice et Bénédict*.

Many of the leaders of the French romantic movement found encouragement for their rebellion in the unrestricted freedom of Shakespeare's plays. Berlioz's own reaction cut to the core of his being: "The pessimistic realism of the tragedies, the structural realism of the histories, the many-sided humor of the comedies, all touched in him an immediate sense of recognition and taught him crucial lessons in artistic freedom and scope."[17] Some critics have suggested that the most striking element of Shakespeare's *Much Ado About Nothing* is its self-conscious use of language, its suggestion of the word as a toy to be played with, to be spoken "truly" or "in sport." Whatever his understanding of English, something of this was obviously apparent to Berlioz, who selected as his final opera's protagonists not Shakespeare's principals, Hero and Claudio, but their satirists, those mockers of convention and appearance, those hardhearted enemies of love (who are eventually gulled into betrothal), the brilliantly witty Beatrice and Benedick. On the structural level the play weaves a counterpoint of two love stories, rather like Berlioz's favorite contrapuntal device of réunion de thèmes, but in the opera he minimizes the misunderstanding of the first couple and treats only the second as they are tricked into an avowal of love. In the fullness of age he surely smiled with approval at Benedick's "For man is a giddy thing, and that is my conclusion," for, in moments of calm reflection, this was surely his conclusion as well.

"Strike up, pipers" reads the last line of the play, one of numerous allusions to music in Much Ado – including that of the title itself, where "nothing," pronounced "noting," can mean not only "observing" but also singing or playing or composing in notes.[18] Was this musical pun available to a Frenchman thumbing through a play called Beaucoup de bruit sur rien? Berlioz was hardly reluctant to use that phrase as a humorous cliché, but he wisely refrained from using it as the title of his opera, for bruit – which may be a good translation of "ado" but which is the common word for "noise" – would have been a far too seductive target for the sarcasm of his detractors.

In fact there is very little noise in the opera, for this is a small-scale work written not for the tumultuousness of Paris but for the tranquillity of Baden. The delight Berlioz experienced while preparing this score, as from October 1860 (well before the opening of Les Troyens), was diminished by repeated illness, but he was able to write "The end" on 25 February 1862, making a few additions, after the first performances, to the published vocal score of 1863. This brief opéra comique, with some of its spoken dialogue taken literally from Shakespeare, has only three arias, two duets and a duettino, two trios, several choruses, and some music for the theater. To the tale of the reluctant lovers Berlioz added his own musical caricature, he told the Princess Wittgenstein, "a grotesque chapel-master named Somarone (a great donkey)," whose asininities – modeled on the those of Shakespeare's Dogberry – lend to the whole an element of farce.

For the nuptials of Hero and Claudio, Somarone has prepared a wedding ode, which he refers to as a *sérénade*, but which Berlioz labels *Épithalame grotesque*. And it is indeed a distorted number, partly because the tunes are short-winded, the rhythms plodding (despite Somarone's claim to have written a gentle hymn to love), and partly because the text is a maladroit parody of the time-honored poetic comparison of death and sexual climax: "Mourez, tendres époux" ("Die, tender spouses"), "mourez, mourez, mourez!" The texture of the piece is that of a double fugue, and, like the "Amen" fugue of *La Damnation de Faust*, it is academically "correct": if the music itself is to produce humor, it must be humorously played.

At the end of the first act of *Béatrice*, Berlioz swings the pendulum away from such horseplay, with its attendant jokes about conductors, and back to the realm of love. The *Duo-Nocturne* sung by the expectant Hero with her lady-in-waiting, Ursula, is one of those supreme moments in Berlioz – the love scenes of *Roméo et Juliette* and *Les Troyens* are others – in which technical mastery and orchestral imagination combine to produce music of unparalleled elegance. Here, a strict poetic construction of closely patterned rhymes in lines of six sylla-bles led Berlioz to music that seems to reveal an intimate and unpre-meditated self, as the opening lines, "Nuit paisible et sereine! / La lune, douce reine" dissolve imperceptibly from the opening key of C sharp minor into the principal key of E major, and, at "Philomèle qui mèle / Aux murmures du bois / Les splendeurs de sa voix," as what sounds as though it might be a four-bar phrase, to mention but one characteristic example of his supple melodic construction, is mag-ically stretched to five.

In 1865 Berlioz reviewed for the Académie des Beaux-Arts a treatise that suggested how all aspects of music could be expressed uniquely by the numbers 1, 2, and 3 and their powers. "I do not believe in the various theories by which one would imprison the art of sound," he wrote. "Music is free; it does what it wants to do – and without permission."[19] The freedom here and elsewhere embodied in Berlioz's music – that supple plasticity, never wild or unrestrained, which none the less perplexed those of his critics who could count only to four – was surely galvanized by his reading of Shakespeare, whose forms and compositional processes inspired so many others in France to rattle the cages of tradition with *contrastes et oppositions* of their own devising. It is somehow gratifying to see the same Berlioz who opened and closed his *Mémoires* with a pessimistic quotation from *Macbeth*, regarding life as a tale that "signifies nothing," closing his musical career with an opera drawn from a Shakespearean comedy that would have the tale of life as "much ado about nothing." Perhaps we should embrace these two perspectives on the world (to cite Berlioz's words about Love and Music) as the two wings of his soul.

Over the years, Berlioz had traveled only rarely to the provinces of France, making forays to Marseilles and Lyons in the summer of 1845, and to Lille in 1846, for the *Chant des chemins de fer*. In June 1859 he had gone to Bordeaux to direct the annual festival of that city's Société de Sainte-Cécile. On a lengthy program there that included arias by Weber, Meyerbeer, Rossini, and Mercadante, sung by local artists and directed by the Grand Théâtre's Louis Costard de Mézeray, Berlioz conducted the *Carnaval romain*, excerpts from *Roméo et Juliette*, and excerpts from *L'Enfance du Christ*. He appears to have exercised upon the players an "electrifying" influence, as the critic of *L'Indicateur* put it, and to have brought to Bordeaux a music that was "exquisite," "luminous," and "inspired."

He was also received like the messiah in June 1863, when he went to Strasburg as the special guest of a grand festival mounted in that border city to celebrate Franco-German relations. Standing on the recently completed railroad bridge that traversed the river from Strasburg to Kehl, Berlioz gave an address proclaiming that love of art had led to harmony among nations: "Such noble love will do far more to advance the complete unification of our two countries than even this magnificent bridge over the Rhine," he said, in words that history would soon prove to be overly optimistic. But the performance of *L'Enfance du Christ* that he conducted in the special auditorium constructed for the occasion was a grand success – the chorus "didn't go flat by even half a quarter-tone," he later reported to Ferrand – and Berlioz was bathed in flowers and applause.

The emoluments had been equally fragrant in April, in Weimar, where Berlioz conducted a performance of *Béatrice et Bénédict*, and they would be sweet again in mid-August, in Baden-Baden, where Berlioz would conduct two more performances of his new opéra comique. But in November 1863, the rewards of seeing *Les Troyens à Carthage* finally performed at the Théatre Lyrique turned out to be bittersweet. Executed each Monday, Wednesday, and Friday night for seven weeks, *Les Troyens* had a *succès d'estime* of twenty-one performances between the première of Wednesday, 4 November, and the last (exceptional) performance of Sunday, 20 December. Alternating with *Les Troyens* at the same theater were Mozart's *Figaro* and Bizet's *Pêcheurs de perles* (about which Berlioz quipped affectionately, in the last review he wrote for the *Journal des débats*, "M. Bizet, a laureate of the Institute, has made the required voyage to Rome. He has returned without having forgotten how to write music."). After the 20th, *Les Troyens* was replaced at the *Lyrique* by a production of Verdi's *Rigoletto*.

At first delighted to witness his work on the stage and to hear the Dido of Anne Charton-Demeur, Berlioz became depressed by the cuts and other indignities the work had had to suffer and by the insufficiencies of those who produced it – something he realized on seeing the work after a three-week absence from the theater caused by a violent case of bronchitis. The traditionalists among the reviewers discussed the libretto more than the score because they could read French but not music; the nay-sayers failed to find in Berlioz what they found in the "classics" – *La Muette de Portici*, *La Juive*, *Les Huguenots*, that is, all three concurrently on view at the Opéra; and the know-nothings, who liked neither *Tannhäuser* nor *Les Troyens*, went round repeating the

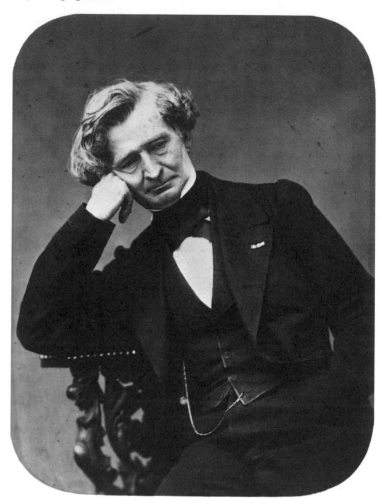

15 One of the four photographs of Berlioz taken by Pierre Petit in the spring of 1863, which Berlioz considered "superior to all the others."

inanity that Wagner was "Berlioz without melody" – hardly a compliment to our composer, who admitted to being ashamed of the secret pain such disparagement caused him. More than a few critics recognized the solemn grandeur of Berlioz's conception, however, and one in particular spoke with especial grace of the moment I have mentioned above. On 15 November Auguste de Gasperini wrote that he had never heard "a more dignified hymn, a more elevated and gentle melody" than that of the Septet in Act 4, "a marvel of science, of meditation, and of inspiration." "Ah, my dear Gasperini," the composer told the critic on the day the review appeared:

> What a style, what a sympathetic understanding of great art – what a beautiful thing is your article in Le Ménestrel. My son has just read it to me, and I am overcome with gratitude. I am ill, and have been in bed for six days. Will you not grant me the pleasure of shaking your hand? Come, I beg you, please come.

Meyerbeer attended five performances of the opera. Berlioz's son Louis attended all twenty-one (the receipts at the gate show that after the third week the house was at most half full)[20] and collected some sixty-four reviews of the production.[21] Some of these predicted a brilliant future for Les Troyens, as did the music-loving painter Frédéric Bazille, who saw the opera several times, bought the score, and played through it with pleasure: "They are no longer giving Les Troyens," he wrote, "but I am certain that it will be taken up again with great success."[22] Such comments lead us to wonder whether Berlioz did not act too hastily in "protecting" his score from further mutilation by withdrawing rather than defending it at the time, in late December, when his star, Mme Charton-Demeur, moved on. (His withdrawal of Cellini, in Paris in 1839 and in London in 1853, might also have been premature.) That he wanted but could not achieve absolute control of the production is evidence of high artistic principle – but it was something inevitably out of step with the manifold practical realities of the contemporary operatic world.

A meaningful legacy

It is tempting to see the actions of artists approaching old age as attempts to sum up the creative endeavors of their careers. Berlioz began early, setting down the first chapters of his Mémoires when he was only forty-four (in the aftermath of the 1848 Revolution). In early

1864, drained by the previous year's performances of *Les Troyens*, the now sixty-year-old Berlioz turned again to the manuscript of his *Mémoires* to add a Postface (after the 1856 Postscript), which resumed ten years' activities, including the gestation and birth of the two last operas, and ended on a sour note:

> I am alone. My contempt for man's folly and baseness and my hatred of his atrocious cruelty have reached a peak of intensity. And I say hourly to Death: "Take me when you will!" What is he waiting for?

Then, in September, he added yet another coda to the book in order to tell of his autumnal encounter with Estelle – the woman who, as a teenager, had first taught him the extremes of feeling, and who, even now, could cause his heart to shiver with remembrances of times past.

After his evanescent devotion to Amélie, in 1862, Berlioz had once again begun to think of this distant beloved, Estelle Dubœuf, now the widow of the prominent Grenoblois lawyer, Xavier-Casimir Fornier. In 1864, he wrote to Estelle, and began a tender if distant relationship that lasted for some four years. "I love her as though she were still young and beautiful," he told the Princess Wittgenstein, and under the heading of "I see Mme F—again; *Convulsions de cœur*," he appended some of their correspondence to the *Mémoires*. The photographs of the elderly Estelle convey no great charm. But we know almost nothing of her manner or of her voice, since Berlioz faithfully executed his promise to destroy her many letters, and these, we do know, provided great comfort to him during his last five years.

On 23 April 1865, Berlioz told the Princess Wittgenstein that he was having the *Mémoires* printed so that Estelle Fornier could read of his life. It is satisfying that the rekindling of love's youthful delights closed not only Berlioz's emotional biography, but also the formal thematic circle of the *Mémoires* – whose clearly rounded super-structure is asserted by the recapitulation on the last page of the quotation from Shakespeare on the first. At the outset we read Macbeth's famous words in French: "La vie n'est qu'une ombre qui passe"; at the end we read them again, in the original: "Life's but a walking shadow." The gesture – opening and closing with the same material – is Haydnesque, but the thought, unlike those of the earlier master, is despondent. The several codas appended to the end, too, are rather evocative of the romantic manner of symphonic construction. Here, as elsewhere, one is led to wonder: did Art imitate Life, or did Life imitate Art?

In the spring of 1865 Berlioz had twelve hundred copies of the *Mémoires* printed at the nearby Imprimerie Vallée, and stored them, unbound, in his office at the Conservatoire. Over the years that were left to him, he must have distributed some fifty of these, as we learn from the contract his heirs signed with their posthumous publisher: Michel Lévy purchased the remaining eleven hundred and fifty copies from the family, in January 1870, for the handsome sum of six thousand francs. (The firm would make ten further impressions of the volume between 1878 and 1930, and would thus more than recover its initial investment).[23] In August 1865 Berlioz took a specially bound and dedicated edition to Geneva, where he had it delivered to Estelle; and he gave a number of copies to close friends and acquaintances, among them the devoted Princess Wittgenstein and the faithful Humbert Ferrand. Was this the last gesture of a dying man, as Berlioz seemed to think?

Not quite. The authors of the revolutionary decrees that led to the foundation of a national conservatory of music thought from the beginning that the institution should have, in addition to a public library, a collection of musical instruments, past and present, in order to put on display some of these "practical tools" from the workshop of the human spirit. Budgetary restrictions, vandalism, sales, and bizarre occurrences such as the burning of some twenty harpsichords to heat the premises, in 1816, impeded the growth of the collection over the early years, and Cherubini's personal need for office space, in 1822, brought it to a halt. Only in 1861, when the composer Louis

Clapisson sold his own instrument collection to the school, for twenty thousand francs, and in 1862, when Clapisson was officially named curator of the collection (at a salary of two thousand francs per year), did the museum get a new shot in the arm.

Shortly after Clapisson died, on 19 March 1866, Berlioz – whose one enduring official title had long been that of Bibliothécaire du Conservatoire – was offered the post of curator. This new sinecure did not carry the free lodging that Clapisson had enjoyed, but it did lead to the doubling of Berlioz's annual salary as librarian from fifteen hundred to three thousand francs.[24] This was a boon to the composer, of course, and not at all a loss for the director, Auber, since Clapisson's salary had been greater than the amount of the increase Berlioz received. One might wish to lament the fact that this was yet another minor administrative post for Berlioz: even Clapisson, albeit briefly, had been professor of harmony, from 31 March 1962 until his death. But Berlioz did play a role in the education of the students at the Conservatoire as a kind of unofficial adviser, and as a judge at the end-of-the-year prize competitions. In *Les Soirées de l'orchestre*, for instance, Berlioz joked about the piano competitions of 1850, when the Mendelssohn G minor Concerto was played so many times in succession that the Érard piano borrowed for the occasion began to play the piece *by itself*, and had to be destroyed in order to be silenced. Also, in the *Souvenirs* of the composer Henri Maréchal, who won the Prix de Rome in 1870, we find a portrait of Berlioz as a sphinx-like loner who served on one of the Conservatoire juries of 1868.[25] Despite his failure to obtain a professorship, then, Berlioz was a figure of whom students at the institution were always aware, and from whom, if primarily by proximity and conversation, they were able to profit.

What everyone might have profited from, had the composer been inclined to make one, was a *catalogue raisonné* of the instrument collection, for as a member of the instrumental juries of the Universal Exhibitions of 1851 and 1855, and as the author of the *Grand Traité d'instrumentation et d'orchestration modernes*, completed in 1843 and reissued in 1855 with an additional chapter on newly invented instruments and a supplement on the art of the orchestral conductor, Berlioz was surely more qualified than any of his contemporaries to describe all the instruments that were known at that time. But when he acceded to Clapisson's post in 1866, Berlioz, often listless and unwell, could not have been expected to launch an inquiry of such an obviously demanding sort.

His health did permit him to accept an invitation to travel to Vienna, in December of that year, to lead the performance by the Gesellschaft der Musikfreunde of *La Damnation de Faust*. The work was received warmly by the public, but coolly by the now powerful Eduard Hanslick (who quite wrongly predicted that Berlioz's *Faust* would soon be buried under the reputation of Schumann's). His health also permitted him to travel to Russia, one year later, invited there by the patroness of the Russian Musical Society, the Grand Duchess Yelena Pavlovna, and apparently persuaded to accept the invitation by the topographer-composer César Cui. In the Saint-Petersburg newspaper for which he was chief music critic, Cui contributed an attractive profile of the Berlioz he met in Paris in the autumn of 1867:

> [Berlioz] is now sixty-three years old. He is extremely sensitive and highly impressionable. His imagination is jaded but his conversation is gracious in the extreme. To look at, Berlioz is handsome and impressive. He has a slender face, a high brow, and a dense and naturally curly head of completely white hair. He has deeply set and penetrating eyes that gleam with intelligence, and a long and fine aquiline nose. A few expressive wrinkles mark his brow and the corners of his mouth. He moves gracefully and is well proportioned.[26]

In Russia, where he gave eight concerts between November 1867 and February 1868 (including one, in Moscow, where the *Offertoire* of the *Requiem* produced the "biggest impact" Berlioz had ever witnessed), he was befriended by Vladimir Stassov, Balakirev, Cui, and others of the new Russian school (who enlisted his support in their battles against the pro-Italians on the one hand and the cult of Wagner on the other), and he netted from his concerts the substantial sum of over seventeen thousand francs. He would have made six times as much had he accepted Theodore Steinway's contemporary offer to give concerts in the United States (and he would have become the first great European artist brought to the new world by the firm). We do not know whether he feared a nasty trans-Atlantic crossing or a naïve American public, but for his last hurrah Berlioz preferred to travel in the opposite direction, which was familiar to him from the excursion of 1847.

I have noted that the Postface of the *Mémoires* closes with acrimony. The *Travels in Dauphiné*, however, close with relief: "Oh, Stella! Now I can die without bitterness and without anger." Might such emotional shifts be due in part to the physical illnesses he suffered over the years? The vicissitudes of Berlioz's soul had long been matched by the discomforts of his body: in his letters to family and friends we read, in the early years, of frequent bouts with a severe and painful sort of tonsillitis; in the eighteen-fifties and sixties, we find countless references to far greater suffering, which he attributed to the affliction of *névralgie*. In contemporary encyclopædias this term is subsumed under the heading of *neurasthénie*, or "nervous exhaustion." The symptoms included hypersensitive skin, insomnia, diminution of sexual appetite, gastro-intestinal difficulties, and severe, generalized, ill-defined pain, sometimes likened to the discomfort of a sash bound too tightly round the body. In Berlioz's day those who suffered from *neurasthénie* were occasionally considered hypochondriacs, or *malades imaginaires*. But his pain was real, and frequently so intense as to confine him for hours and even days to his bed. He tried the standard treatments of steam baths and blood-letting, and he tried the more novel techniques of electrotherapy and homeopathic medicine, but the only thing that seems to have brought him temporary relief was laudanum, that commonly used tincture of opium with which his father, too, had attempted to quiet the pains of his own waning days.

To the common-sensical remedy of a mild and regular diet, Berlioz seems to have been uncommonly allergic. As soon as he felt well, he indulged in rich food, champagne, and cigars – even knowing, as he must have, that he would soon suffer the consequences. But the pleasures of the table seem to have put him in a cheerful frame of mind. The composer Julius Stern tells us of a dinner at Meyerbeer's at which Stern's own irritation with Berlioz (for dismissing one of his compositions without a glance) was turned to affection when all those present had, at Berlioz's insistence, consumed several bottles of champagne: "I like him a lot," said Stern; "he is amiability incarnate."[27] As late as 1868, presiding over a choral festival in Grenoble, Berlioz told his Russian friend Stassov that he had been able "to eat, to drink, and to paint the town red." Such comments lead us to wonder whether Berlioz really experienced the early closing of the book of life that some of his biographers have described. There is no doubt, however, that after attending the ceremonial meeting of the five academies at the Institute, on 6 January 1869, and for the remaining two months of his life, the composer remained largely confined to his bed.

Berlioz had established a last will and testament on 29 June 1867, impelled to do so by the receipt, three weeks earlier, of the terrible news of the death of his son. "Great men should probably not have sons," Thomas Mann's troubled son Klaus wrote in 1933, and we may wonder whether Louis Berlioz thought likewise when he reflected upon the home he had known as a youth. Raised at first by French servants and sent off to boarding school in Rouen at twelve, Louis eventually pursued a professional career in the French navy and merchant marine. In the autumn of 1853 he took an examination to become midshipman aboard the steamship Le Corse, the successful results of which Berlioz proudly reported to his sister Adèle in a letter of early October 1853. The evaluation of Louis's work by ship's captain, M. d'Estremont Maucroix, was more dispassionate:

Conduct and morality: good. Complexion: delicate. Aptitude for the seafaring profession: average. M. Berlioz brings to the office of midshipman both enthusiasm and good will. He is only at the beginning of his career, but I believe that he will succeed. [28]

Louis served on various vessels, in commerce and in combat (he was among the combined French and British forces who took the Russian fortress of Bomarsund, in the Baltic Sea, on 16 August 1854, during the Crimean War), and he eventually attained the rank of lieutenant-commander. Sometime before 1861 he was again promoted, and it was as captain of the steamship La Sonora, in Havana, that Louis Berlioz died of the yellow fever, two months before his thirty-third birthday, on 5 June 1867.

Louis had never married, although an English friend of his mother, a Mrs. Lawson, who "loved him as her own son," had tried to make an advantageous marriage for him with a young woman of her acquaintance, one Berthe Frosmont, in December 1859.[29] Nothing came of this association, but Louis does seem to have had an intimate relationship with a young woman from Le Havre, one Zélia Mallet, who had a daughter named Clémentine. Assuming that he was Clémentine's father, Zélia's mother wrote to Louis in April of 1864 to ask what his intentions were regarding the little girl, and requesting that he provide a copy of her birth certificate.[30] Modern genealogical research has so far turned up nothing regarding this or any other child of Louis Berlioz, and the fact that he made his father his sole beneficiary, in his will, suggests that Louis apparently had no children. This would be substantiated if, as it seems, Berlioz made no effort to seek out Louis's progeny, something he presumably would have done at the time of Louis's death if he had known of their existence.[31] It is none the less possible that Louis was the father of Clémentine Mallet but that he was reluctant to recognize the child because of the inferior social status of both the mother (a repasseuse) and the grandmother. (Berlioz himself, it will be remembered, was accused of such class bias by his friend

Tajan-Rogé, at the time of his liaison with the Russian seamstress.) It is thus at least possible that there is a continuing direct line of succession from the composer.

In personal correspondence, Jacques Barzun offers the following postscript to this mystery:

> When my father [a French magistrate] was pulled out of the trenches to assist in administering military justice, around mid-1915, there came before him a young man whose features gave my father an uncommon shock: he was looking at a young Berlioz, complete with reddish hair, aquiline nose, and deep-set eyes, and his name was *something* (I have forgotten) *dit* Berlioz. The use of *dit* is official and not unusual for aliases or even pseudonyms – Poquelin, *dit* Molière. Questioned, the young soldier knew nothing about his name, or would admit nothing. The puzzle remained unsolved.

The will that Berlioz established on 29 July 1867 is revealing of his generous and meticulous soul. Having no known direct descendants, his three nieces became his heiresses, and came into possession of his investment savings and his properties in the Isère. He established a small income for Estelle Fornier, and, in a codicil signed on 12 June 1868, he added a lump sum to the already generous provisions he had made for his mother-in-law, who, after Marie's death in 1862, had continued to live with him and to look after his domestic affairs. He specified what should be done with the copies of the *Mémoires* that he had had printed, and requested that they be translated into German by Susanne Cornelius (the composer's sister), who was certain to avoid the misinterpretations that "infested" the translations of his earlier collections of essays. (This did not come to pass.) He left the autographs of his operas to the library at the Conservatoire, and his books and batons – the traditional mementos of a conductor's affection – to a few close friends. He had already bestowed his own performance parts and scores upon the Société des Concerts, in March 1863, saying that this was "the sole musical institution in France whose prospects for the future inspire confidence in a composer."

Berlioz died in his fifth-floor apartment at 4, rue de Calais, at 12:30 pm, on 8 March 1869. Marie's mother, his companion for the last seven years, saw to the funeral arrangements, to the rent, and to the wages of his manservant and his cook. Shortly thereafter, Mme Sotera de Villas sought lodgings elsewhere. The only mother-in-law that Berlioz had ever known died at her home in the rue Montyon, at age eighty, on 6 June 1876. Nothing in her will suggests that she still possessed items of musical interest.

Berlioz's funeral took place on 11 March, at the Église de la Trinité, with musical selections from his *Requiem* and those of Mozart and Cherubini. The Allegretto of Beethoven's Seventh Symphony and the march from Gluck's *Alceste* were also performed for the occasion, and as postlude, the organist played a transcription of Berlioz's *Marche de pèlerins*. In attendance were Auber, Gounod, Ernest Reyer (who soon acceded to Berlioz's post at the *Débats* and to his chair at the Institute), and other dignitaries from the Conservatoire, the Opéra, and the Institut de France. In behalf of that august fraternity, the sculptor Eugène Guillaume gave a thoughtful address:

> Messieurs, Berlioz will remain one of the great symbols of our century. Few artists are predestined, as he was, to epitomize the period in which they have lived. By the elevation of his aspirations, by his love for the most unfettered and pure wellsprings of art, by his veritable cult of a consummate ideal founded upon truth, he was one of the most vigorous representatives of the new spirit of the age. He was also modern by the notion he contrived of the artist himself, and by the particular character of his own originality. And he was modern as well by dint of a sensibility that took delight in its own sufferings, and that found ingenious ways of rendering them more colorful and profound.

The monetary value of Berlioz's estate was calculated by two notaries and a municipal appraiser, who examined the contents of Berlioz's rooms and papers in the presence of the executors of his will (the organ manufacturer Édouard Alexandre and the composer

Berthold Damcke) and the three members of his family who became his heirs – Mathilde Masclet, née Pal (the daughter of Berlioz's sister Nanci and Camille Pal), who had married Jules Masclet, a lawyer at Grenoble, in 1855; Joséphine Suat (the daughter of Berlioz's younger sister Adèle and Marc Suat), who had married Marc Chapot, a military officer stationed in Vienne, two years earlier, in 1867; and Joséphine's sister Nanci, still unmarried, who was represented by a notary. This official party returned to Berlioz's lodgings on six different occasions during the month of May 1869 in order to witness the official evaluation of his worldly goods, of which many had come to him at the time of his marriage to Marie Récio. The grand piano that Pierre Érard gave to Berlioz in February 1851 was still there, as was the bronze statuette by Antoine-Louis Bayre that the Duchesse d'Orléans had offered to him in gratitude for having dedicated the Symphonie funèbre to her husband, in 1842. Two large engraved portraits of the Emperor Napoleon and the Empress Eugénie were hanging in the salon, and several hundred books and scores were spread over two adjoining rooms. (We do not know what became of them.)

For one interested in the painstaking process by which French wills were executed in the eighteen-sixties, the detailed inventory of Berlioz's possessions makes fascinating reading.[32] Suffice it to say here that the total worth of his property and his investments came to just under one hundred and sixty-three thousand francs: this is nearly three times the value of the average estate of the Parisian who left a will in the period after mid-century. If many of Berlioz's letters lead us to believe that he was only one step away from indigence, this sum helps to explain how he none the less kept two households, a servant, a cook, and a professional schedule that required suitable clothing and constant travel. Indeed, an examination of his entire financial picture suggests that from allowances from his father, the prize stipend, employment at the Conservatoire, commissions, income from concerts, inheritance, investments, journalism (which paid for the groceries, as D. Kern Holoman has remarked), and profits from publication (which I believe paid the rent)[33] – in other words, from his family and from a broad range of musical tasks and obligations, Berlioz did manage to maintain an honorable, middle-class existence.

Do I make too much of money in this study? If you read the section of *My Life*, Wagner's autobiography, that concerns his first visit to Paris, you will not think so. The melody or accompaniment of Wagner's every thought – even when he sings, hilariously, of losing and finding his dog – is inflected with the sharps and flats of cash. But in the Postscript of the *Mémoires* Berlioz specifically rejects the notion that a love of money had anything to do with his love of art: "Should one offer me a hundred thousand francs to sign my name to one of those works that are today immensely successful, I would angrily refuse. That is how I am made." Berlioz's music demonstrates the truth of this proposition.

Afterword

The Maginot line

"It may be said without exaggeration that from the death of Rameau up to about 1870, French music ceased to exist." When Jean Aubry wrote those words in 1917, in *An Introduction to French Music*, he did make an exception for Berlioz , but only with the mixed assessment that he was a "literary composer" and "an imperfect genius," whatever that may mean. The technique of parenthetical disparagement in the service of praise – ultimately demeaning, all too frequent in popular writing on Berlioz – should forever be eschewed, I think, for its impact can be stultifying, and long-lived. I feel comfortable hearing of Berlioz's "conspicuous uniqueness" (Jacques Barzun's phrase), but find assertions of his "oddity" disturbing when they suggest that it is somehow of an unmusical sort. If Berlioz does not swim in the channel of the "main stream" of music, to use Tovey's lasting if oft-criticized metaphor, it is because that stream was carved out by historical forces hardly free from prejudice.

In his *Reflections of a Nonpolitical Man*, Thomas Mann asked, mischievously, "Can one be a musician without being German?" Nineteenth-century orchestral music has long been seen as an essentially Germanic unfolding of which the *fons* if not the *origo* was Beethoven. This complex phenomenon has much to do with a developing and powerful German nationalism, whose consequences were felt, at home and abroad, in realms well beyond the purely political, and well into the twentieth century – for the arts, none more than music, were deeply joined to the sense of German identity, even if the Germans, and nearly everyone else, invariably took Paris to be the capital of Europe. Those of all musical persuasions continued and continue to suckle at Beethoven's breast and to study with professors never weaned from that pleasure. Beethoven's style – the mature, "heroic" style – became not only institutionalized as "normal" and "main-stream," but the very "daylight by which everything else must be night," as Scott Burnham has nicely put it in a recent monograph appropriately entitled *Beethoven Hero*.[1] If this exaggerates the propensities of today's off-campus listeners, it is no less the case that the modern Berliozian, like the modern Rossinian, for example, and even the modern Schubertian, must hope that thoughtful critics will continue to search for tools that can find value in genres and procedures quite different from – even when inspired by – those employed by the composer of the Ninth Symphony.

In addition, admirers must confront the fact that Berlioz was listed, as early as 1859, as a member of the triumvirate, with Wagner and Liszt, that headed a so-called *Neudeutsche Schule*, or New German School. Now, Berlioz did of necessity become a *European* composer, and this is one reason that it is appropriate at the present time, when *Europe* is the magic word in political discourse on the continent, to bring his life and work to the fore. But the label "German" is on its very face absurd, since two of the three composers mentioned are not *deutsch*. Still, the tag – which was coined as an epithet for the progressive party of music by Franz Brendel, editor of the *Neue Zeitschrift für Musik* – gained momentum and support, partly because it was immediately attacked by another group of serious-minded musicians among whom were the violinist Joseph Joachim and the youthful Johannes Brahms. Brahms's group believed that music was grounded in inalienable principles and timeless laws, while those of the New German School (whether or not they accepted Brendel's nomination) allowed the composer's inner experience to take precedence over, to question, to modify and even to reject the canons of tradition; they urged concomitantly that the ultimate judgment of the contemporary work of art be rendered by those of a more or less distant future.

In his philosophical essay on *Harold en Italie* for the *Neue Zeitschrift für Musik*, which appeared in that magazine exactly twenty years after Robert Schumann fired the opening salvo of German Berlioz reception with a brilliant analysis of the *Fantastique*, Franz Liszt made this explicit, obviously hoping to find future justification not only for Berlioz's work, but also, of course, for his own. Berlioz was less inclined to theorize about the frontiers of new music than were his German contemporaries, including his friends Hans von Bülow, Richard Pohl, Peter Cornelius, and others of the "school," some of whom are now better known for their Wagnerolatry than for the high esteem in which they held Berlioz. Had he read German, however, Berlioz would have found knowledgeable appreciation from them of the ways in which he, too, had moved symphonic music in the direction of poetry, and hence towards that future of which the *Neudeutschen* dreamed.

"If you're a German you can't stand the French, but you like to drink their wines all the same," wrote Goethe in *Faust*. Berlioz's treasure was not precious wine but progressive music, and despite Goethe's remark – which is in fact satirical – the composer and his work, well into the twentieth century, found many sympathetic friends on German soil.

Richard Wagner and the future of music

After hearing *Roméo et Juliette* at the end of 1839, Wagner, not yet the composer of *Der fliegende Holländer*, felt as though he were again a "mere schoolboy":

> This was a completely new world for me, in which I had to try to find my way in an unprejudiced manner commensurate with these impressions. At first it was the impact of orchestral virtuosity, such as I had never before dreamed of, that nearly overwhelmed me. The

fantastic boldness and sharp precision with which the most
audacious orchestral combinations pressed almost tangibly upon
me, over-awed my own musico-poetic sensibility and drove it with
irresistible force back into my innermost being. I was all ears for
things I had until then had no conception of and which I now had to
try to explain to myself.[2]

That Wagner, years later, when dictating his memoirs to Cosima,
remembered the moment in this uninhibitedly positive way – despite
the mixed feelings he had by then developed about both the man and
his music – is testimony to the force of those first Parisian impressions, when he came to know Berlioz as the composer of the four symphonies from the *Fantastique* to the *Funèbre*. Of these, *Roméo et Juliette*
finds particular echo in *Tristan und Isolde*, from the creation of the small
"magic casket" motif to the larger conception of the hero's "delirium." Wagner seems openly to have acknowledged the debt when he
presented Berlioz with the extraordinarily generous gift of the first
copy of the full score, inscribed "Au grand et cher auteur de *Roméo et
Juliette*, l'auteur reconnaissant de *Tristan et Isolde*."[3]

It was also in Paris that Wagner came to know three Jews of
unequaled prominence at the time, the composers Fromental Halévy
and Giacomo Meyerbeer, whose *La Juive* and *Les Huguenots* were regularly on the boards at the Opéra after their creations in 1835 and 1836,
and the music publisher Maurice Schlesinger, for whom Wagner
worked in various capacities during his first sojourn in France. He
recounts a conversation at Halévy's home in which someone asked
Schlesinger if he was a Jew, and was told that he had been born Jewish,
but that he had become a Christian out of respect for his wife. Adds
Wagner: "The casual manner in which this subject was discussed
astonished me pleasantly, for in Germany any such conversation
would have been anxiously avoided for fear of offending the person
concerned." It would be a cruel irony if this sort of informality worked
on Wagner as an incentive to express his own ill-starred thoughts on
the matter, but it is possible that one of his less than honorable fuses
was indeed lit in the French capital.

Richard Wagner's antipathy to Jews and its relation to his artistic work are issues of continuing debate in the broader worlds of historical and cultural study. Did the composer inscribe into the fabric of his music dramas the disdain that he expressed in his anonymous pamphlet *Das Judentum in der Musik* (*Jewishness in Music*), first published in 1850 and reissued, with his name attached, in 1869? Or was he able to rise above personal prejudice when creating the masterpieces of art that continue to this day to fascinate opera lovers everywhere? Wagner remains the leading candidate for chief musical villain of all time because of what subsequent generations, and most notably the specific figure of Adolf Hitler, made of his work and his person. Indeed, the megalomania of the one has been associated with, and even attributed to, the other.

The larger problem for the critic is to identify not the nazified Wagner, not the de-nazified Wagner, not even the "Wagnerian" Wagner, but, in so far as is possible, Wagner *tout court*. Now, no movement ever attached to Berlioz – or to Beethoven, for that matter – the way Wagnerianism attached to Wagner. But if we wish to maintain that Berlioz, like Wagner, is one of the seminal figures of the musical nineteenth century, then this particular beacon ought to be directed upon the French composer, too, in order to see him in the light that makes even admirers of the German's music abhor the man. There is sufficient evidence to make an informed investigation.

Berlioz's first important publisher was Wagner's nemesis, Maurice Schlesinger, who brought out Berlioz's original Opus 1, *Huit Scènes de Faust*, and later, the *Fantastique*, the *Requiem*, the *Symphonie funèbre*, and a host of works of lesser dimension. A letter that Berlioz wrote to Schlesinger from Italy, in December 1831, gives evidence of an already easy relationship between the twenty-eight-year-old composer "in exile" and the thirty-three-year-old German immigrant who was Berlioz's neighbor in Paris, and who soon became, in correspondence, not "mon cher Schlesinger," but rather the more intimate "mon cher Maurice." That Berlioz took over the editorship of the *Revue et Gazette musicale* when Schlesinger was absent from Paris, in the summer of 1836, suggests, again, nothing but harmonious relations with this Jewish entrepreneur whom Wagner, in one of his kinder epithets, called a "lecherous old goat."[4]

Berlioz's relations with Meyerbeer – the paramount target of the arrows of Wagner's *Das Judentum in der Musik* – were similarly cordial. Berlioz seems to have genuinely admired much of the older man's music; and Meyerbeer's regular attendance at *Les Troyens* in 1863 was the last of many signs of his own considerate regard for the work of the French composer. Although Berlioz had more mixed feelings about the music of Halévy, he had many regular contacts with the composer of *La Juive*, at the Opéra (where Halévy was an assistant conductor), on official commissions, and in the press. Apart from some innocent wordplay regarding the titles of the operas *La Juive* and *Le Juif errant*, there is not a shred of evidence that Berlioz's feelings about the man or about his music, which were lukewarm until 1856, when they became colleagues at the Institute, were in any way influenced by Halévy's religious background.

In an age in which open hostility to Jews was not uncommon – signs of it can be found in Chateaubriand, Victor Hugo, Vigny, and Balzac, for example, as well as in the writings of some of the early socialist thinkers of the day – Berlioz would seem to have rejected it out of hand. In his review of Wilhelm von Lenz's *Beethoven et ses trois styles* (the book I mentioned in the Introduction that credited its author with the already established "theory" of Beethoven's three style periods), Berlioz reproaches Lenz for the following observation regarding Mendelssohn:

> One cannot speak of modern music without naming Mendelssohn-Bartholdy. [. . .] We take a back seat to no one in demonstrating the respect that a mind of such caliber deserves, but we think that the Hebraic element by which Mendelssohn's thinking is colored, as everyone knows, will impede his music from becoming the property of the whole world, without distinction of time or place. [. . .] The Jews are often among the best when it comes to acquiring technical facility or energetically applying concepts that have been learned.

This results from the fact that the accomplished man is far more the
faithful echo of his learning than the expression of his individuality,
while the performer, and especially the composer, *can* and *should*
express *nothing* but his own nature.[5]

Here Lenz would seem to be echoing Wagner's *Das Judentum in der
Musik* of two years earlier (though he does not mention that article,
which was itself the by-product of a continuing debate), where
Mendelssohn is specifically accused of stringing together "highly
polished, refined and craftsmanlike figures" which leave our "higher
sensibilities" "untouched."[6] Be this as it may, Berlioz, to whose writings Lenz plays explicit homage in his book, and on more than one
occasion, had the courage to write as follows:

> Is there not a little prejudice involved in this way of judging that great
> musician, and would M. Lenz have written these lines had he not
> known that the composer of St. *Paul* and of *Elija* was a descendant of
> the famous Jew Moses Mendelssohn? I find this hard to believe. "The
> psalmodies of the synagogue," he goes on to say, "are the prototypes
> of what one finds in Mendelssohn's music." Now, it is difficult to
> imagine how the chants of the synagogue can have influenced Felix
> Mendelssohn's musical style, since he never practiced the Jewish
> religion. On the contrary, everyone knows that he was a Lutheran,
> and a fervent and sincere one at that.
>
> Moreover, what kind of music could ever become the *property of the
> whole world, without distinction of time or place*? None, most certainly.
> The works of the great German masters such as Gluck, Haydn,
> Mozart, and Beethoven, who all belonged to the Catholic – that is, the
> "universal" – religion, will no more achieve universality than the rest,
> no matter how wonderfully beautiful, vibrant, hearty, and powerful
> they may be.[7]

With characteristic brevity and principle, Berlioz – who sees the Jew as
an exponent of a religion, not an exemplar of a race – explicitly rejects
the notion of universality that pollutes many an aesthetic debate, and
sweeps aside as absurd and irrelevant the platitudinous Judeophobia
of Lenz and, in the process, of Wagner as well. Would that others had

done likewise. But in an age that saw Jews as outsiders in all realms other than that of commerce – the sole realm in which they were widely permitted to work, as too many tend to forget – Berlioz's words were far from common. It turns out that the Dreyfusards of a future generation, when French anti-Semitism reached the peak of a crescendo, might have looked to Berlioz for musical support.

German anti-Semitism reached a climax in the second quarter of the twentieth century, and the name of Richard Wagner was closely linked to those responsible for the rise and fall of the Third Reich – one of the reasons that his name remains so provocatively alive today. The Holocaust has rendered discussion of the issue more sensitive than almost any other, yet discussed must it continue to be, for it remains an open question as to whether Wagner's philosophical cant led to his adoption by the Nazis or whether the Nazis' peculiar passion for art led to their adoption of Wagner. For Berlioz the issue cannot be framed so neatly, but the generally strong support that he expressed for leaders of the July Monarchy and Second Empire, which stands in contrast to the weakness he experienced in the operatic arena that was the key to success, demonstrates that in France, too, as I have suggested here, the politics of art require explanation in terms that include the artistic taste of the politicians.

In the purely musical arena, Wagner remains alive as the initiator of the "music of the future" – the name of a treatise, "Zukunftsmusik" (the quotation marks are a part of the title), that first appeared in France (and in French) as a *Lettre sur la musique*. This was the preface to the publication of four of Wagner's librettos translated into French prose by his friend Frédéric Villot, a curator at the Louvre; it was a manifesto designed to support *Tristan und Isolde* and his newly "Tristanized" *Tannhäuser* by explaining the mentality of a German composer working in the face of the powerful Italian and French traditions, and to persuade readers of the justice of his cause: the creation of a new kind of ideal yet profoundly human form of art.

I believe an argument can be made that one reader whom Wagner wished particularly to persuade by his writing was Berlioz, for both composers were grappling with the conflation of symphonic and dramatic values which they found in Beethoven (and, earlier, in Gluck), and which they wished, each in his own way, to employ themselves. What might have become a productive discussion never materialized, however, for Berlioz was understandably embittered by the imperial favor granted to *Tannhäuser* at the Opéra, which pushed aside consideration of *Les Troyens*, and he was delighted at the scandalous reception of the Wagner, which caused the composer to withdraw the score after only three performances. On this occasion Berlioz turned his weekly column over to Joseph d'Ortigue, believing that his silence would articulate his disapproval even more eloquently than his words.

If Berlioz could have heard *Tristan* and *The Ring*, would he have enjoyed the musical references to *Roméo et Juliette*, his own "music of the future," as I would call it, uniting a Beethovenian symphonic edifice with a literary conception of high dramatic import? Would he have been gratified that Wotan's D flat major awakening in the opening scene of *Das Rheingold* seems to echo the nobility of first entrance of the Pope, in the same key, in the third Tableau of *Benvenuto Cellini*? Or that the anvils struck behind the scene during the descent into Nibelheim seem to echo those heard during the chorus ("Bienheureux, les matelots") of the *Cellini*'s fourth Tableau, which are likewise *derrière la scène?* Such resonances, of which one could easily list more, suggest that Wagner did indeed pay Berlioz the high compliment of making a thorough study of his musical works. Berlioz returned the favor by reading closely through the score of *Tristan* that Wagner gave him and marking in pencil those places that struck a dissonant chord. The chromaticism that Richard Wagner here raised to the level of principle was simply overbearing to the French composer, who preferred ambiguities at the more modest level of the individual melodic phrase.

Wagner's appearances in Paris in 1860 and 1861 – the scandal of *Tannhäuser* and its concomitant caricatures and parodies – led to the providential response to the opera of Charles Baudelaire, who, in an essay that appeared in the *Revue Européenne* entitled "Richard Wagner et

Tannhäuser à Paris," appreciated the decadent sexuality and larger emotional effects of Wagner's music, and who thus launched what might be called the "age of Wagner" in France. This age also witnessed a simultaneous attempt, in the aftermath of the Franco-Prussian War, to glorify the unique musical genius of the specifically French tradition, and to "de-Wagnerize" the French musical landscape. And there were ardent admirers of both, among them the painter Henri Fantin-Latour, who created a series of original lithographs for Adolphe Jullien's magnificently illustrated biography of Berlioz, which appeared in 1888. (The original drawing of the last of these is preserved in the collections of my own institution. See illustration 16.)

There is far more to the story of Berlioz and Wagner than can be told here, and their many encounters form an object lesson in nineteenth-century musical aesthetics. Richard Wagner long theorized about music for the people but came eventually, like Berlioz, to regard the general public with a certain disdain. None the less these two men were of very different temperaments, for Berlioz was a man whose customary behavior and whose work were principled in like degree. Berlioz usually lived up to his artistic achievements, in other words, while Wagner did not, for even those who claim that Wagner's mature works are exemplary cannot say the same of his character.

Wagner's *musical* influence – in Germany, in France, throughout Europe and beyond – was profound (this is precisely what Brahms feared), while Berlioz's was far more limited. Liszt, of course, was a partisan. Félicien David's descriptive symphonies Le Désert (1844) and Christophe Colomb (1847) surely owe debts of gratitude to Roméo et Juliette and La Damnation de Faust, as does Ernest Reyer's opera Sélam (1850); Peter Cornelius said that his Barber of Baghdad (1858) was inspired by Benvenuto Cellini; I hear echoes of Béatrice et Bénédict in the Act 1 duet of Édouard Lalo's Le Roi d'Ys (1888); others hear echoes of L'Enfance du Christ in Debussy's Le Martyre de Saint Sébastien (1911), and in Honneger's Le Roi David (1921). In matters of orchestration Berlioz was an inspiration to generations of Russian composers (Stravinsky

16 *Hommage à Berlioz*, a preparatory drawing for one of the fourteen original lithographs that Fantin-Latour made for Adolphe Jullien's *Hector Berlioz, sa vie et ses œuvres* (Paris, 1888). To the right of the central figure of the muse, holding a scroll with the titles of the principal works, we see Marguerite (from *La Damnation de Faust*) fastening a wreath to the tomb, Dido (from *Les Troyens*) facing Marguerite's back, Juliet (with a veil) facing Romeo, and, in the foreground, Fantin himself, holding a celebratory crown of flowers.

said that he was "brought up" on Berlioz) as well as to Richard Strauss, who generously revised Berlioz's *Traité d'instrumentation* (by "Wagnerizing" it) in 1904, and to Gustav Mahler, whose song-cycles are clear descendants of the orchestral version of Berlioz's *Nuits d'été* (and whose performances of the *Fantastique* in New York simply electrified the critics). Edgard Varèse appreciated Berlioz, and Olivier Messiaen, who knew most of the music, always spoke admiringly of Berlioz's inventive sonorities. The American composer George Crumb has suggested that among those he had in mind when working on his electronic string quartet, *Black Angels*, was Berlioz. For Crumb, and for other contemporary composers, the Frenchman's name may be as much a symbol of a certain kind of compositional freedom as it is an abbreviation for the totality of his œuvre.

What is missing here are the names of Berlioz's younger contemporaries and immediate successors – Charles Gounod, Ambroise Thomas, Georges Bizet, Jules Massenet – whose paths cannot be said to have emanated from that of the composer of *La Damnation de Faust*. However, Camille Saint-Saëns, whom Berlioz befriended and highly esteemed, wrote that his entire generation had been educated by the *Traité d'instrumentation*, and well educated at that, because the book had the invaluable merit of inspiring the imagination. Saint-Saëns' recollections of the composer are among the most revealing documents we have from the post-Berlioz generation.

Last judgment

Some of those who saw Berlioz late in life – Henri Maréchal, for example, who won the Prix de Rome in 1870; Ernest Reyer, who succeeded Berlioz at the *Journal des débats* after Joseph d'Ortigue's brief tenure there as music critic; Eugène Guillaume, who gave the eulogy at Berlioz's funeral in behalf of the Académie des Beaux-Arts – remembered him as frail, tormented, and overcome with despondency. That he long suffered from neuromuscular afflictions and, in his sixties, from the other pains of old age, is hardly surprising. But I continue to wonder if so many such recollections have tended overly to darken our image of his last decade, which seems to stand in stark contrast to the fire and brimstone we associate with his youth. Another winner of the Prix de Rome, Louis Bourgault-Ducoudray, found Berlioz ebullient and even "volcanic" as late as 1862, and for his concert tour in Russia of five years later Berlioz clearly drew on wells of passion and energy that were far from dry. To the end, Berlioz was one of those men whose language – verbal and body – reflected his moods with especial vigor; psychological tension and physical illness only reinforced the highly emotional character that was his from the beginning. Pauline Viardot said as much in 1859 when, worried that Berlioz's admiration for her had suddenly turned to love, she noted that high emotion had a fatal effect on him: "toute émotion le tue."

When a first volume of Berlioz's correspondence appeared in 1878, Émile Zola's friend Henry Céard suggested that Zola write an article on a man who, like himself, fought in his reviews against mediocrity and official stupidity and, frustrated at the end, cried out that he could write no more.[8] Céard, too, likening Berlioz to Beethoven and to Balzac, promulgates a one-sided view of the composer – as though all had been in vain. Camille Saint-Saëns, writing to Berlioz's biographer, Adolph Boschot, was more realistic:

> I saw Berlioz often and liked him very much, and I do not quite recognize him in the portrait that he left of himself. Obviously, when one is young, such exaltation and exaggeration are not at all surprising. But an entire life of rage, sorrow, delirious enthusiasm, praise and condemnation pushed to the utmost extreme – is it really true? Or is there not in all of this a healthy dose of literature? He speaks of a little rehearsal of *Armide*, for which I was at the piano, and he says that "we were suffocating" with admiration. Now, I remember the occasion quite well; we were indeed much taken by the music of Gluck, and we were unquestionably moved. But we were certainly not "suffocating."
>
> I saw a lot of Berlioz because I admired him and I liked him very much, but I would not have visited him so often if he had really been the man he depicts himself as having been. Highly excitable myself, I could never have endured such constant exhilaration.[9]

Saint-Saëns knew Berlioz as a proselytizer for the love of beauty. But he also knew him, when they were preparing *Armide* for the Théâtre Lyrique in January 1866, for example, as a "working stiff" – a practical composer and conductor concerned with getting the notes played correctly and in tune.

This, the unromantic pragmatism of the systematic composer and the methodical conductor, is too often forgotten. In 1854, preparing to give a concert with Joseph Joachim, concertmaster to the King of Hanover, Berlioz urged his colleague to "remind the first oboe that he must bring his English horn," and to "make sure that the bass clarinet – the instrument, not the man – is in good shape." Such unsentimental episodes in the life of the artist must be underlined if we wish to support the claim that Berlioz was often as far from the outlandish fanatic described in his own prose as he was from the freak described by his critics; the claim, in short, that he was the outstanding musician of his day.

In his hilarious novel *Talking It Over*, Julian Barnes has a character mention that "Radio 3 in the background was churning out something by one of those Bachs who weren't Bach"; later he notes that "There was a Haydnish sonata, a gentle piano tracking up and back in patterns which you could half anticipate even if you'd never heard the piece before." Here we have a wry commentary on eighteenth-century music not entirely lacking in truth. But for the nineteenth century that will not do. There was only one Berlioz, and because it is impossible to "half anticipate" his patterns, the word "Berliozish" will find resonance nowhere. His art is unique because, apart from its intrinsic merits, much about it seems curious, even inconsistent, yet extraordinary and attractive, and therefore tempting to try logically to elucidate. Now, a great modern Berliozian, Pierre Citron, has suggested that it is *dangerous* to be logical when one concerns oneself with Berlioz. This is the sort of wit that Berlioz would have liked – for its *sound* if not its sense. In fact, no matter how logically we may attempt to interpret it (as logically as possible, I should think), the mystery of high art will always escape reduction to an array of pronouncements or to a set of propositions.

On the market of historical reputation, Berlioz's stock will remain volatile and precarious, I am afraid, because his art requires of the public a preparation tantamount to that of the performers who bring it to life. This old idea, which the great violinist Pierre Baillot mentioned to Berlioz's English friend John Ella, was voiced at a time when the audience for art music was growing, and at a time when listening to art music was considered an art. In those precincts where it still is, Berlioz's stock will rise – because of the astonishing originality and uncommon radiance of his music, which reflects an imagination addicted to expression and exasperated by complacency; because of the irrepressible wit and timeless wisdom of his writings, which demonstrate a principled respect for authorial wishes far ahead of its time; and because of the distinctive intermingling of art and life that is striking to all who attend even casually to Berlioz's career, and that is, cast upon the broader plane, a central concern of all modern aesthetic inquiry.

Introduction

1 Berlioz makes this point explicitly in the little biographical sketch he
   sent to Dieudonné Denne-Baron, in May 1852. See Berlioz,
   Correspondance générale, IV, ed. Pierre Citron, Yves Gérard, and Hugh
   Macdonald (Paris: Flammarion, 1983), pp. 163–165. Unless
   otherwise indicated, quotations from Berlioz's letters here are from
   this edition.

2 The notion was articulated in Paris as early as 1827, in the *Revue
   musicale*, by François-Joseph Fétis – who may have acquired it from
   Beethoven's first biographer: see Johann Aloys Schlosser, *Beethoven:
   The First Biography* [1827], ed. Barry Cooper, transl. Reingard Pauly
   (Portland: Amadeus, 1995).

3 Immediately after Boschot's book appeared, Théodore Dubois,
   newly retired as director of the Conservatoire, went so far as to
   wonder why the author of a three-volume study would go to such
   pains to ridicule the subject of his research. The manuscript of
   Dubois' review of Boschot's biography is preserved in the archives of
   the Académie des Beaux-Arts of the Institut de France; I H 16.

4 In his autobiographical *Vie de Henry Brulard*, Stendhal, who was born
   not far from Berlioz's home town, in the Département de l'Isère,
   mentions a local grocer whom he identifies as "Reyboz or Raybaud,"
   the uncertain spelling evidence that the author would have
   pronounced both names in the same way, without sounding the final
   consonant (*Vie de Henry Brulard* [Paris: Gallimard, 1973], p. 128).

Concerning the possibly silent final consonant of Berlioz's name, one might also wish to suggest that the composer referred to the partly autobiographical artist-hero of the sequel to the *Symphonie fantastique* as "Lélio," an otherwise curious choice, precisely because of that name's faint similarity to his own.

1 Initiation

1 *The Memoirs of Hector Berlioz*, transl. and ed. David Cairns (London: Cardinal, 1990), p. 5. My quotations from the *Mémoires* are from Cairns's highly readable translation, which I have sometimes modified (without indication) in accordance with the original text as presented in Hector Berlioz, *Mémoires*, ed. Pierre Citron (Paris: Flammarion, 1991).

2 Russell Jones, "Americans in Paris 1825–1848: the medical students," *Laurels*, 57 (1986–87), 169–180.

3 See V. Donnet and C. Moureaux, "Le baccalauréat-ès-sciences d'Hector Berlioz," *Marseille Médical*, 106/3 (1969); the article "baccalauréat" in *La Grande Encyclopédie*; and I. Grattan-Guinness, "A note on Hector Berlioz and the Université Royale de France," *Music Review*, 50 (1989), 181–184.

4 This manuscript is preserved in the Pierpont Morgan Library in New York.

5 See Peter Bloom, "Berlioz to Ferrand: Eight *Billets intimes*," *Musical Quarterly*, 79 (1995), 574.

6 Archives Nationales (henceforth AN), AJ[37] 208.

7 AN, AJ[37] 3(5), 81.

8 Archives de l'Assistance publique, Hôpitaux de Paris (Berlioz's letter to the hospital administrator; 25 October 1829).

9 *Correspondance de George Sand*, ed. Georges Lubin, vol. 4 (Paris: Garnier, 1968), p. 248.

10 The award was made in 1826. See AN, O[3] 1305.

11 See AN, F[4] 2926.

12 This becomes clear from Fétis's articles in the *Revue Musicale*, 6 (January 1830), 571, 588–590.

13 AN F[21] 610 and 611.

14 Académie de France à Rome, Carton 34 (31 December 1830).

15 AN, AJ¹³ 187 (III).

16 AN, O⁴ 1327. Berlioz's little-known letter to His Royal Highness is preserved here along with one from Harriet Smithson regarding the performance she was to give on the same day (mentioned below).

17 Archives de l'Opéra 12 [2, No. 5], 27.

18 AN, AJ¹³ 1059.

19 AN, O⁴ 1327.

20 L'abbé Clerc-Jacquier, *Histoire de La Côte-Saint-André* [1853], p. 169.

21 *Édition de la Pléiade*, XI (Paris: Gallimard, 1990), p. 172.

2 Innovation

1 *My Life*, transl. Andrew Gray (Cambridge, 1983), p. 39.

2 *Ludwig Börne: A Memorial*, in Heine, *The Romantic School and Other Essays*, ed. Jost Hermand and Robert Holub (New York: Continuum, 1985), pp. 275–276.

3 Berlioz, *Correspondence Générale*, I, p. 445; letter of 6 May 1831. Chactas is the narrator of Chateaubriand's *Atala*.

4 Henri Peyre, "Shakespeare's women – A French view," *Yale French Studies*, 33 (1964), 107–119. Actually Peyre wrote "*brainless* angels of purity."

5 This is suggested by Charles Forster, *Quinze ans à Paris (1832–1848)*; cited by Lloyd Kramer, *Threshold of a New World* (Ithaca: Cornell, 1988), p. 19.

6 I published the marriage contract in *Cahiers Berlioz*, 2 (1995) (La Côte-Saint-André: Association Nationale Hector Berlioz, 1995).

7 Preserved in Louis's dossier at the Service historique de la marine; CC7 Alphabétique 172.

8 Archives de Paris, Fichier des mariages parisiens, vol. 17.

9 Bibliothèque Nationale de France (henceforth BNF), Berlioz, Lettres autographes. The letter is sketched on the back of Berlioz's draft of the program of the concert of 25 November 1838.

10 Ernest Deldevez, *La Société des concerts* (Paris, 1867), pp. 6–7n.

11 Sand, *Lettres d'un voyageur* (Paris, 1971), p. 311.

12 All writers have believed that Berlioz's last article was the review of Bizet's *Les Pêcheurs de perles* that appeared in the *Journal des débats* on 8 October 1863. Thanks to a clue provided by David Cairns, I would suggest that the humorous piece in the *Revue et Gazette musicale* of 20 August 1865, "Coups de boutoirs" (signed "X") is by Berlioz. Further articles by Berlioz may well be lurking in the pages of that magazine.

13 Friedrich Blume, in *The Creative World of Mozart*, ed. Paul Henry Lang (New York: Norton, 1963).

14 In the metaphorical sense, Berlioz was correct; in the practical sense in which he was speaking – sponsorship of the publication of the score – it was not the state, but the subscriptions, that covered the expenses of Maurice Schlesinger's first edition of 1838.

15 The finest snuff, called *poudre d'hospice*, was reserved at the time for medical use.

16 AN, F²¹ 4633 (5).

17 *Le Charivari*, 12 September 1838. His daughter Louise's *Esméralda* was premiered at the Opéra in November 1836.

18 AN, AJ³⁷ 67.

19 AN, F²¹ 1292.

20 Adam, *Lettres sur la musique française*, ed. Joël-Marie Fauquet (Geneva: Minkoff, 1996), p. 144.

21 Adam, *Lettres*, p. 144

22 BNF, Berlioz, Papiers divers, No. 12. "Martin" appears at no. 33 of the "Chœurs, Dames."

23 See Peter Bloom, "La Mission de Berlioz en Allemagne," *Revue de musicologie*, 66 (1980), 70–85.

24 On this subject see Joël-Marie Fauquet, "Hector Berlioz et l'Association des artistes musiciens," *Revue de musicologie*, 67 (1981), 211–236; and Fauquet, "L'Association des artistes musiciens et l'organisation du travail de 1843 à 1853," in *La Musique et le pouvoir*, ed. Fauquet and Hugues Dufourt (Paris: Aux Amateurs de livres, 1987), pp. 103–124.

25 Hanslick's 1846 essay is quoted in Geoffrey Payzant, *Eduard Hanslick and Ritter Berlioz in Prague* (Calgary: University of Calgary, 1991).

26 In *Le Faust de Berlioz* (Paris: Costallat, 1910), Adolphe Boschot takes the work as a whole to be Berlioz's portrayal of the "romantic soul," and, citing text in the libretto that Berlioz did not set (that Faust, "peut-être," would be saved), he suggests that the conclusion – like that of Goethe's text and of Wagner's *Ring des Nibelungen* – exemplifies the Christian notion of redemption through love.

3 Introspection

1 Nigel Gosling, *The Adventurous World of Paris 1900–1914* (New York: William Morrow, 1978), p. 7.

2 The petition is preserved in AN, F²¹ 956.

3 AN, O³ 1619 (I), the *Règlement* of the Society.

4 BNF, Berlioz, Lettres autographes, vol. VII.

5 The complete letter, as yet unpublished, is preserved in AN, F²¹ 1306.

6 *Registre des personnels administratif et enseignant 1822–1901*, No. 95 (Centre de Documentation, Conservatoire National Supérieur de Musique de Paris).

7 See Ella's letter to Charles Hallé, 3 November 1854, in *The Autobiography of Charles Hallé* (London, 1896), pp. 249–250.

8 AN O⁵ 53, No. 2018.

9 Adolphe Adam, *Lettres sur la musique française*, p. 751.

10 David Cairns very kindly provided me with the texts of these letters, which are preserved in the Collection Reboul.

11 AN, F¹² 5018 (Alexandre's dossier in the archives of the Légion d'honneur). The letter is undated, but must have been sent on 14 or 15 July 1857, since it was received and date-stamped at the Ministry on 16 July.

12 That is, Aeneas himself, born of Aphrodite – the "Cytherean" – on the isle of Cythera.

13 From a notebook preserved in the Musée Berlioz. The annotation was made before Berlioz left for Gotha, on 30 January 1856.

14 This letter, dated 21 May 1858, was kindly put at my disposal by Richard Macnutt.

15 Victorin Joncières' description, from *Notes sans portées*, quoted in *Wagner et la France* (Paris: Herscher, 1983), p. 26.

16 This letter is preserved in the Musée Berlioz.

17 See Katherine Reeve Kolb, "Hector Berlioz," in *European Writers: The Romantic Century*, vol. 6 (New York: Scribner's, 1985), p. 777.

18 James Wey, "Musical design in *Much Ado About Nothing*," in *Twentieth Century Interpretations of Much Ado About Nothing*, ed. Walter Davis (Englewood Cliffs: Prentice-Hall, 1969), p. 86.

19 Archives de l'Académie des Sciences; quoted in Peter Bloom, "*Berlioz à l'Institut* Revisited," *Acta Musicologica*, 53 (1981), 196–197.

20 AN, AJ^{13} 459.

21 Thirty-four of these are given in Frank Heidlberger, ed., *Hector Berlioz, Les Troyens à Carthage, Dossier de presse parisienne* (Saarbrücken: Lucie Galland, 1995).

22 Frédéric Bazille, *Correspondance*, ed. Didier Vatuone (Montpellier: Les Presses du Languedoc, 1992), pp. 68, 78.

23 The Berlioz dossier in the Calmann Lévy archives gives the precise dates and press runs: March 1878 (1500 copies); May 1881 (1000); March 1887 (1000); September 1896 (1000); February 1904 (1000); March 1911 (500); March 1919 (500); June 1921 (1000); June 1926 (750); November 1930 (1000). A note indicates that the stock was exhausted after 1938.

24 AN, AJ^{37} 67; *Registre des personnels administratif et enseignant 1822–1901*, No. 95 (Centre de Documentation, Conservatoire National Supérieur de Musique de Paris). The decree authorizing Berlioz's accession to the post is dated 4 April 1866.

25 Selections from these *Souvenirs* are translated by Hugh Macdonald in the *Berlioz Society Bulletin*, 155 (1996).

26 Quoted by Alexandre Bourmeyster in "Berlioz et ses héritiers russes," *Silex*, 17 (1980), 102.

27 See Richard Stern, *Erinnerungsblätter an Julius Stern* (Leipzig, 1886), p. 51.

28 Service historique de la Marine (see chapter 2, note 7).

29 This information comes from letters of Louis Berlioz preserved at the Musée Berlioz.

30 The letter from Mme Mallet (kindly provided to me by David Cairns) is preserved in the Collection Reboul.

31 The latter point was made to me by Berlioz's great-great-great niece, Catherine Reboul-Berlioz, in a thoughtful communication for which I am deeply grateful.

32 Hervé Robert and I published this and other documents in "A propos de la vie matérielle et de la condition sociale d'Hector Berlioz: l'apport des actes authentiques," *Cahiers Berlioz*, 2 (1995).

33 See my "Episodes in the livelihood of an artist: Berlioz's contacts and contracts with publishers," *Journal of Musicological Research*, 15 (1995), 219–273.

Afterword

1 (Princeton: Princeton University, 1995), p. 155.

2 *My Life*, p. 191.

3 BNF, Musique, Rés. vm3 5.

4 *Selected Letters of Richard Wagner*, transl. and ed. Steward Spencer and Barry Millington (New York: Norton, 1987), p. 125.

5 Wilhelm von Lenz, *Beethoven et ses trois styles* (Paris: Legouix, 1909), pp. 43, 46. I have quoted two sentences more than Berlioz does in *Les Soirées d'orchestre*.

6 Wagner's essay appears in English in *Wagner*, vol. 9, no. 1 (1988).

7 Berlioz, *Les Soirées de l'orchestre*, ed. Léon Guichard (Paris: Gründ, 1968), pp. 399–400. These comments appeared in Berlioz's article for the *Journal des débats* of 11 August 1852.

8 Henry Céard, *Lettres inédites à Émile Zola*, ed. C.-A. Burns (Paris: Nizet, 1959), p. 60; cited in Émile Zola, *Correspondance*, ed. B. H. Bakker (Montréal, 1982), p. 259.

9 Quoted in Saint-Saëns, *Regards sur mes contemporains*, ed. Yves Gérard (Paris: Coutaz, 1990), pp. 17–18. Berlioz wrote "nous étouffions" in the letter to Ferrand of 17 January 1866, which Saint-Saëns would have read in the *Lettres intimes* of 1882.

Works by Berlioz

D. Kern Holoman's *Catalogue of the Works of Hector Berlioz* was published in 1987 as volume 25 of the *New Berlioz Edition*. For information about each work's title, required performing forces, dating, sources, and performance during Berlioz's lifetime, this is the place to start.

Authoritative scores – scores, that is, that give the most accurate possible readings based on comparison of all available sources – can be found in the *New Berlioz Edition*, published in Kassel by Bärenreiter under the general editorship of Hugh Macdonald and found in research libraries everywhere. The introductions to these volumes (in English, French, and German) offer information of the sort found in the Holoman *Catalogue*, but in considerably fuller terms, and the critical notes give details about the differences among the autograph manuscripts in Berlioz's hand, the copyists' manuscripts, and the various published editions. Included in the back matter are facsimiles of the composer's manuscripts that demonstrate his handsome calligraphy and his attentiveness to detail. For Berlioz, this new "critical" edition is of especial importance because the earlier, standard edition, published by Breitkopf und Härtel at the beginning of the twentieth century, is riddled with errors.

Anyone with further interest in Berlioz must read his last book. The best edition in the original language is Hector Berlioz, *Mémoires*, présentés et annotés par Pierre Citron (Paris: Flammarion, 1991). Of the *Mémoires* there is a magnificent English edition translated and edited by David Cairns, *The Memoirs of Hector Berlioz*, published variously by Victor Gollancz Ltd. in 1969, by W. W. Norton in 1975, and most recently by Cardinal, in 1990.

Berlioz published three collections of his own criticism and miscellaneous essays: *Les Soirées de l'orchestre* (1852), *Les Grotesques de la musique* (1859), and *A Travers chants* (1862). These were reissued in Paris by Gründ, excellently edited by Léon Guichard, in 1968, 1969, and 1971. Of the first there is an unsurpassed translation by Jacques Barzun, *Evenings with the Orchestra* (Chicago: University of Chicago, 1973), now out of print. Of *A Travers chants* (whose title is a pun on *à travers champs*, which means something like "tramping across the fields," and which might be rendered as "through fields of song"), there is a recent translation by Elizabeth Csicsery-Rónay published as *The Art of Music and Other Essays* (Bloomington: Indiana University, 1994).

A critical edition of Berlioz's letters, under the general editorship of Pierre Citron, is now nearing completion (six volumes take us to 1863, a seventh will take us to 1869, and a supplement, I hope, will present additions and corrections): Hector Berlioz, *Correspondance générale* (Paris: Flammarion, 1972–). Of the selections from his letters that have appeared in English translation, the most important are *New Letters of Berlioz*, transl. and ed. Jacques Barzun (Westport: Greenwood, 1974) – a bilingual edition; and *Selected Letters of Berlioz*, ed. Hugh Macdonald, transl. Roger Nichols (London: Faber and Faber, 1995) – in English only. For those in search of a life in letters, Macdonald has supplied concise connective tissue.

Berlioz's *Grand Traité d'instrumentation et d'orchestration modernes* was first published in 1844; to the second edition, published in 1855, Berlioz added a manual on conducting – *L'Art du chef d'orchestre* – that was also sold at the time as a separate brochure. The treatise originally appeared without musical examples, rather like a serialized novel, in sixteen separate installments of the *Revue et Gazette musicale*, from 21 November 1841 to 17 July 1842. These have recently been gathered and reissued as Hector Berlioz, *De l'instrumentation*, ed. Joël-Marie Fauquet (Paris: Le Castor Astral, 1994). Some libraries possess the English translation of the *Treatise* made in 1855 by Mary Cowden Clarke. Hugh Macdonald has made a new translation for publication by Cambridge University Press.

Biographies

The principal biographies of Berlioz in English are those by Jacques Barzun, *Berlioz and the Romantic Century* (3rd edn., New York and London:

Columbia University, 1969), David Cairns, Berlioz. *The Making of an Artist*
(London: André Deutsch, 1989), D. Kern Holoman, *Berlioz* (Cambridge,
Mass.: Harvard University, 1989), and Hugh Macdonald, *Berlioz* (London:
Dent, 1982). To these may be added Peter Raby's *Fair Ophelia. Harriet
Smithson Berlioz* (Cambridge, 1982).

Of Hugh Macdonald's 1982 life and works for Dent's *Master Musicians*,
which replaced the earlier, uneven volume by J. H. Elliot, of 1938, a
wrong-headed reviewer wrote that "Jacques Barzun may rest easy,"
entirely missing the point, for neither Macdonald (who fitted his
comprehensive knowledge to the confines of that series), nor anyone
else for that matter, including Cairns (whose 1989 biography, elegantly
written and lovingly detailed, is the first of a two-volume study), and
Holoman (whose thorough and technically informed study is directed
at the experienced musician), has attempted to duplicate Barzun's
inimitable feat. When Barzun wrote, in the nineteen-forties, most
listeners' notions about Berlioz were more wrong than right, for the
music was little known and sparsely recorded, and had a home in no
reliable edition. Now recordings are legion, and Macdonald is bringing
to completion the authoritative *New Berlioz Edition*. The music was listed
in no comprehensive thematic register. Now we have Holoman's fine
Catalogue. There was no complete edition of Berlioz's numerous, often
delightful and always informative letters. Now we have a *Correspondance
générale*. Only Berlioz's criticism – his newspaper articles and reviews, of
which there are nearly a thousand – remains unavailable in a satisfactory
form. The first of a projected ten-volume complete edition appeared as
this book was being drafted: Hector Berlioz, *Critique musicale*, 1, ed. H.
Robert Cohen and Yves Gérard (Paris: Buchet/Chastel, 1996).

Recent studies of the period

The practical realities of daily life at the court of Louis-Philippe, the
monarch with whom Berlioz was most familiar, are nicely laid out in
Anne Martin-Fugier, *La Vie quotidienne de Louis-Philippe et de sa famille*
(Paris: Hachette, 1992). In *La Musique en France des Lumières au Romantisme,
1789–1830* (Paris: Flammarion, 1986), Jean Mongrédien surveys the
teaching of music, the music of the French Revolution, the principal
French theaters, and sacred and instrumental music, thus achieving a
broad picture of music in France at the dawn of Berlioz's career as a

composer. Mongrédien's book has recently appeared as French Music from
Enlightenment to Romanticism, transl. Sylvain Frémaux (Portland:
Amadeus, 1996).

Recent studies of the music and the writings

Brian Primmer's The Berlioz Style (London and New York: Oxford
University, 1973), which may be read by the conscientious general reader,
speaks elegantly and admiringly of Berlioz's handling of melody,
tonality, and harmony in the effort to demonstrate that the Berlioz style is
deeply expressive, carefully premeditated, and logically contrived. The
analytical reductions of Julian Rushton's The Musical Language of Berlioz
(Cambridge, 1983), and his highly perceptive comments on matters
related to voicing, texture, rhythm, and form, are directed to the reader
with advanced musical training. Katherine Reeve Kolb's essay on
"Hector Berlioz," in European Writers: The Romantic Century, vol. 6 1(New
York: Scribner's, 1985) is a subtle appreciation, by a person with great
literary expertise, of Berlioz the writer (of texts musical and literary) in
the context of the romantic generation in France.

Collections of essays

Berlioz Studies, ed. Peter Bloom (Cambridge, 1991), contains highly
detailed articles on matters biographical, analytical, and aesthetic by
leading Berlioz scholars from France, England, and the United States.
Presentations from the Colloque Hector Berlioz of October 1975, ed. Pierre
Citron, appear in Romantisme, vol. 12 (1976) and, ed. Yves Gérard and Jean
Gribenski, in the Revue de musicologie, vol. 63 (1977), and include
discussions (in French) on all aspects of Berlioz's creativity by an
international group of specialists. Le Conservatoire de Paris, 1795–1995, ed.
Anne Bongrain and Yves Gérard (Paris: Buchet/Chastel, 1996) contains
articles (in French) on Cherubini's directorship, on Habeneck and the
Société des Concerts, and on the library and the instrument collection,
where Berlioz was an administrator from 1839 until his death. Music in
Paris in the Eighteen-Thirties, ed. Peter Bloom (Stuyvesant, N.Y.: Pendragon,
1987) contains twenty-two articles (in French and English) on Berlioz
and the musical world around him in the Paris of his most fertile decade.
La Musique en France à l'époque romantique, 1830–1870 (Paris: Flammarion,

1991) is a collection of articles (in French) on the pianists and violinists, the instrument makers and the press, and the opera and chamber music of the period of Berlioz's maturity.

I have said in the Introduction that non-French scholars remain in the forefront of Berlioz research. However, for treatment of the broader issues regarding political activities, artistic currents, and musical institutions, the points of view of French scholars must be given particular weight.

For further research

Since the appearance of Jeffrey Langford and Jane Graves's *Hector Berlioz. A Guide to Research* (New York and London: Garland, 1989), a highly useful annotated bibliography of over a thousand books and articles (written from Berlioz's day to the late nineteen-eighties) nicely organized into thirteen individual categories, more water has flowed over the dam. A supplement will appear in *The Cambridge Companion to Berlioz*, ed. Peter Bloom (forthcoming).